TWAYNE'S WORLD AUTHORS SERIES

A Survey of the World's Literature

Sylvia E. Bowman, Indiana University
GENERAL EDITOR

FRANCE

Maxwell A. Smith, Guerry Professor of French, Emeritus
The University of Chattanooga
Former Visiting Professor in Modern Languages
The Florida State University

EDITOR

BORIS VIAN

(TWAS 293)

TWAYNE'S WORLD AUTHORS SERIES (TWAS)

The purpose of TWAS is to survey the major
writers—novelists, dramatists, historians, poets,
philosophers, and critics—of the nations of the world.
Among the national literatures covered are those of
Australia, Canada, China, Eastern Europe, France,
Germany, Greece, India, Italy, Japan, Latin America,
New Zealand, Poland, Russia, Scandinavia, Spain, and
the African nations, as well as Hebrew, Yiddish, and
Latin Classical literatures. This survey is complement-
ed by Twayne's United States Authors Series and
English Authors Series.

The intent of each volume in these series is to present
a critical-analytical study of the works of the writer;
to include biographical and historical material that
may be necessary for understanding, appreciation,
and critical appraisal of the writer and to present all
material in clear, concise English—but not to vitiate
the scholarly content of the work by doing so.

Boris Vian

By ALFRED CISMARU

Texas Tech University

Twayne Publishers, Inc.   ::   New York

Library of Congress Cataloging in Publication Data

Cismaru, Alfred, 1929-
  Boris Vian.

  (Twayne's world authors series, TWAS 293. France)
  Bibliography: p.
  1. Vian, Boris, 1920-1959.
PQ2643.I152Z615 1974   848'.9'1409   73-17214
ISBN 0-8057-2951-8

MANUFACTURED IN THE UNITED STATES OF AMERICA

This Book Is Dedicated

to

My Wife

Preface

When Boris Vian died in 1959, hardly anyone knew him in this country. In France, very few had paid attention, before his death, to the obscure novelist, playwright, jazz trumpeter, song writer, ballet and opera composer, slightly Existentialist and overly Pataphysician mystifier and jester; after all, he had to be some Russian immigrant, or descendant of a Russian immigrant trying too hard *to belong*, to appear French, to make a name for himself.

As this book is going to press, *aficionados* of literature in the United States not only have heard of Vian, but have read him, as the highly successful translations of his works published by Grove Press began to hit the market a few years ago. Vian's sporadic appearance on and off Broadway, the translations mentioned above, as well as his presence in a number of anthologies and readers in use in American colleges and universities, point to the prominent position he is beginning to occupy on the contemporary literary scene. While the sexuality to be found in many of his works, and his always mordant anticlericialism and antimilitarism have attracted a dubious mass public, the genuine student of literature suspects, and the researcher finds the intrinsic, intricate validity of his very personal, if very peculiar mythology.

Although not even half of his literary production is available in English, in France in particular, but in all of Europe in general, his reputation continues to increase because the reading and viewing public is beginning to be introduced to the real Boris Vian, to the man behind the mask, beyond the façade of the Prince of Saint-Germain-des Prés, as his friends and followers called him. Yet, in spite of the fact that the posthumous limelight cast upon the author remains largely unequaled in the history of twentieth-century French letters, there is no single book in English dedicated to the writer. There are very few critical comments on him, mostly occasioned by the publication of a translation or by the rare presentation of one of his dramas. The present study intends to fill a lacuna in the scholarship on Boris Vian by discussing all his novels, two representative short stories, and all the plays with the exception of his musical comedies, none of which has been staged so far. Because of space limitations, the following works will not find commentary herein: *Barnum's Digest, Cantilènes en gélée* and *Je voudrais pas crever,* collections of poetry of little literary consequence; *En avant la zizique,* an essay on music; *Textes et chansons,* a collection of lyrics; and *Manuel de Saint-Germain-des-Prés,* a polemical essay.

Because of the unavailability of some novels and plays, and because of the limited circulation of others in this country, it has been deemed necessary to provide the reader, on occasion, with rather detailed summaries and frequent quotations. The latter, always in translation, should make for a more effortless understanding of Boris Vian's often cryptic but always brilliant preoccupations and themes. For the sake of clarity, a division by genre has been adopted: the novels are examined first, both those which appeared under his own name and those published under the pseudonym of Vernon Sullivan, followed by a discussion of the short stories and of the plays. Since both his life and his work are extremely complex and defy categorization, the text is preceded by an introductory chapter designed to *explicate* Vian and, hopefully, to unravel a few myths largely dispelled in France, but still persisting in this country.

Texas Tech University

ALFRED CISMARU

Contents

Chronology

1920   March 10: Boris Vian born at Ville-d'Avray; second of four children. At age twelve he becomes a cardiac patient.

1933   Student at Lycée Hoche in Versailles.

1936   Student at Lycée Condorcet in Paris.

1938   Becomes an *aficionado* of jazz after listening to the concerts of Duke Ellington who visits France; learns the trumpet.

1939   Student at Ecole Centrale; gives up playing the trumpet because of cardiac difficulties.

1941   Marries Michelle Léglise.

1942   Becomes a member of and plays in the Abadie orchestra; birth of a son, Patrick; enters employment of AFNOR as engineer.

1946   Begins to write articles on jazz in *Combat* and *Jazz-Hot;* quits AFNOR; *J'irai cracher sur vos tombes,* novel.

1947   *Vercoquin et le plancton, L'Automne à Pékin, Les Morts ont tous la même peau,* and *L'Ecume des jours,* novels; begins to write translations and will continue to publish them up to his death.

1948   *Barnum's Digest,* collection of poems; *Et on tuera tous les affreux,* novel; Court proceedings against him prompted by scandal of *J'irai cracher sur vos tombes;* birth of a daughter, Carole.

1949   *Les Fourmis,* collection of short stories; separates from his wife and begins to live with Ursula Kübler, a dancer.

1950   *Elles se rendent pas compte* and *L'Herbe rouge,* novels; *Cantilènes en gelée,* collection of poetry; *L'Equarrissage pour tous* and *Le Dernier des métiers,* plays.

1952   Enters the College of Pataphysicians; divorces Michelle Léglise.

1953   *L'Arrache-coeur,* novel.

1954   Marries Ursula Kübler.

1955   Becomes Artistic Director for the Jazz Division of Philips; begins to compose the melodic themes and words for a number of songs, and by the end of his life he will accumulate some four hundred such compositions.

1956   Cardiac and lung complications.

1958   *Fiesta,* opera libretto; *En avant la zizique,* essay.

1959   *Les Bâtisseurs d'Empire,* play. June 23: dies while viewing a film version of *J'irai cracher sur vos tombes.*

1962   *Les Lurettes fourrées,* posthumous collection of short stories; *Le Goûter des généraux,* play published by his friends at the College of Pataphysicians; *Je voudrais pas crever,* posthumous collection of poetry.

1965   *Théâtre I,* containing *Le Dernier des métiers, L'Equarrissage pour tous* and *Le Goûter des généraux.*

1966   *Textes et chansons,* collection of lyrics; *Trouble dans les Andains,* novel.

1971   *Théâtre II,* including *Tête de méduse, Série blême,* and *Le Chasseur français,* unstaged musical comedies.

CHAPTER I

Vian the Man

IN the poem entitled *Je voudrais pas crever,* which provides the title for the collection of poetry published by Pauvert, Vian wrote:

> I shall die a little, much,
> Without passion, but with interest,
> And then when all shall be finished,
> I shall die.[1]

In fact, by the time he died in 1959, Vian did experience the progressive aspect of death which modifies and steers the existence of chronically ill persons. The constant presence of the threat of physical annihilation infused the author with an urgent vitality which resulted in what one critic called *La Poursuite de la vie totale,*[2] and another *Les Vies parallèles de Boris Vian.*[3] This vitality prompted him to complain in the largely autobiographical *L'Herbe rouge:* "I lost sixteen years of my life in sleep," pointing, of course, to the necessary, if wasteful, periods of rest in one's life.

Because Boris Vian did in fact rest very little, and because his multifarious careers are at times difficult to trace, it may be convenient to separate an examination of his life into three divisions. The first will consider his childhood and teen years; the second will review his career as novelist and playwright within the context of his other activities; while the last few years, those which followed his second marriage, will constitute the topic of the third division.

I *From Ville-d'Avray to Paris*

Boris Vian was born on 10 March 1920, in the little town of Ville-d'Avray near Paris. He was the second of four children. His father, Paul Georges Vian, was eight years younger than his mother, Yvonne Vian, and perhaps because of the unusual chronological age difference between his parents, Vian's early years were spared those family friction episodes which so often mar and influence the temperament of many children. Yet, if he was witness to no unusual parental arguments, neither was he the object of any particularly wholesome home life, as is apparent from numberless comments which he made later on this subject. "There is no such thing as a good parent," he is reported to have said. "All parents are the same...in so far as the thickness of blood is concerned, I don't believe in it."[4] In the already quoted *L'Herbe rouge* he explained: "Never have they beaten me.... One could not make them angry. To make them angry, you had to do it on purpose. It was necessary to trick them into it. Every time I felt like being upset, I had to make believe I was." One thing which perhaps he held against his parents was their choice of *Boris* as a first name. Many during his life, and some even after his death, believed him to be of Russian or Armenian origin, and it is possible that during his childhood days he had to suffer the little cruelties which some French children often launch in the face of a *métèque*. Later, to his friends, he had to explain often that *Boris* had nothing to do with his national origin: his parents simply happened to like that name. No matter though, for on many occasions he used a variety of pseudonyms: Baron Visi, Vernon Sullivan, Adolph Schmürz, and others.

According to Yvonne Vian, her husband was a good, generous, and tolerant man. It is known that in politics he was liberal and in religion he was savagely anticlerical; both of these characteristics are readily discernible in his son. It is possible also that Boris' penchant for translating works from English is another inclination which he inherited, for Paul Georges Vian himself did a number of such translations. His good nature and his literary interests notwithstanding, it is also a matter of record that his father had little concern for finding permanent employment or for providing his family with a stable financial security. The economic situation of the Vians deteriorated, especially in the early 1930's, and there is therefore little wonder that in several of Boris' works one notes the fall from rich to poor of many personages. His father's death in 1944, during the troubled days of the liberation period, when he became the mysterious victim of a rather enigmatic assassination, was certainly a blow to Boris, who never found out who was responsible, nor the exact circumstances which led to the murder. A certain amount of tardy investigation proved that Paul Georges Vian was not killed because of collaboration with the occupying German forces, for indeed there is nothing to point to it; his death was obviously the result of an unusual if still mysterious set of circumstances of the type for which only war in general can be rendered guilty.

In 1932 Boris Vian has a touch of rheumatic fever, and his heart is affected. This event, of course, is going to determine to a great extent the rest of his life. From 1932 to 1936 he attends Lycée Hoche in Versailles, but his studies are interrupted in 1935 by another health problem. He becomes ill with typhoid fever, the doctors are reported to treat him badly, he takes a long time to recover, and he develops an insufficiency of the aorta. Nevertheless, in the course of the same year, he passes his Latin-Greek Baccalaureate, and in 1936 he is able to enter the Lycée Condorcet in Paris where he pursues mathematical studies in preparation for admission at the Ecole Centrale. Still, the illness affected his family life immediately, for he soon had to bear the burden of motherly solicitude. His resentment of maternal love, carried to the extreme, has been expressed in a number of books later on. In *L'Herbe rouge,* for example, he stated: "I was being drowned in love. I was loved too much; and as I did not love myself, I concluded logically the stupidity of those who loved me. . .their bad intentions even." While he recognizes that, according to the usual criteria, his parents had been good to him, he goes on to accuse them of cowardice because, by taking on their shoulders the entire responsibility for his bad health, they did not allow him to lead the life of a normal child, nor to find for himself the external limits of his physical condition. In the same work he states:

When I looked out a window, I was not allowed to bend; I could not cross the street by myself; whenever the wind would start to blow, I had to put on my winter coat whether it be winter or summer, and I could never take off my wool sweater. . . . My health was something terrible. Up to age fifteen I could only drink boiled water. But the cowardice of my parents consisted in the fact that. . .they made me, in the long run, fear for myself, they made me tell myself that I was fragile. . . .During all of my childhood, my father and my mother have taken on their shoulders everything that could possibly hurt me. Morally, I felt a very strong embarrassment about it, but my softened flesh hypocritically enjoyed it all. . . .Then I was ashamed of myself, ashamed of my parents, and I hated them.

When questioned on these details by David Noakes, Madame Paul Vian is reported to have explained: "If we took a great deal of care of Boris. . .it is because he really needed it."[5] Furthermore, Madame Vian was shocked when certain critics attempted to identify her with the monstrous mother of *L'Arrache-coeur.* Nevertheless, Boris explains in *L'Herbe rouge* what was the direct consequence of his mother's extreme solicitude: "I would get away in order to appear that I was elsewhere. . .little by little I built around me a world of my own. . .without sweaters, without parents. Empty and luminous like a boreal landscape, and I wandered in it, tireless and tough, the nose up in the air and the eyes looking straight forward."

Yet, his diseased body could not endure any sustained efforts. His mother and wife recall the heart palpitations, the periods of extreme fatigue, and Vian himself, in the unpublished "Les Cent Sonnets," remembered that he would often "catch the croup after having a cold." However, if Vian objected to the maternal care to which he was subjected in his teen years, it is noteworthy also that he modified later his opinions on parenthood when his own son, Patrick, reached the age of seven. In 1948 he became acutely aware of his own paternal obligations. While Michelle Léglise opines that her husband always detested such responsibilities and considered them as weighing too heavily on him, the fact is that, after his divorce, he insisted on seeing his children regularly, and he is reported to have worried and cared about Patrick's education and even to have threatened intermittently to place him in some Jesuit school if he did not straighten out. It is possible, as his second wife suggested to me, that the image of the father in *L'Arrache-coeur* and *Les Bâtisseurs d'empire* is due in part to Vian's tardy modification of his ideas on parenthood, and also, that the father described in these two works represents Boris Vian equally well.

Be it as it may, Vian's early childhood appears to have been largely uneventful, while his teen years were marred in part by lack of financial security, in part by health problems. The latter appear also to have resulted in excessive maternal domination, and to have given to the author an unusually acute taste for freedom, a taste which was going to remain in his innermost fibers for the rest of his life.

II   *From Music To Literature To Music*

It was in 1937 that Boris Vian began to be interested in jazz and to learn the trumpet. In the course of the same year he became a member of the Hot Club of France, and that is also when he went to listen to a concert of Duke Ellington who was then touring Europe. Ellington's concert was both an experience and a revelation. In fact, later, Vian counted the concert as one "of the three great moments of (his) life,"[6] the other two having to do also with jazz, namely the concert of Dizzy

Gillespie to which he listened in 1948, and that of Ella Fitzgerald in 1952. For him, music meant jazz, and Duke Ellington, as well as Louis Armstrong, represented the best in the medium. It is reasonable to deduce that it is through jazz that Vian became acutely interested in the United States, as his translations of various American authors indicate. While he never visited the United States in person, he always followed closely the developments in American music especially, but also American external politics and internal, racial problems.

In 1939 Vian passes the entrance examination at Ecole Centrale: he places 125th in 313 admissions. Because of his heart ailment he is not mobilized when the war begins. Owing to the hostilities, the class to which he was assigned moves from Paris to Angoulême. In the course of the following summer, at Cap-Breton where his family took refuge, Boris makes the acquaintance of Michelle Léglise who was there with her family for similar reasons. In August, 1940, his parents return to Paris, and Vian continues his studies at the Ecole Centrale, while at the same time he courts Michelle Léglise whom he is going to marry on 3 July 1941, in a civil ceremony at first, and religiously two days later. It is in the course of the same year that he first tries his hand at literature by beginning work on the unpublished "Les Cent Sonnets."

The role of Michelle Léglise in Vian's literary beginnings cannot be exaggerated: "At the origin, it was in order to amuse Michelle that Boris began to write," stated Michel Rybalka.[7] Michelle was only three months younger than Boris, and they were both only twenty. During the first year of marriage, and until 1943 when she was operated on, Vian's wife had thyroid problems which affected the normal course of her pregnancy. She would not have borne her child too well, were it not for the fact that her young husband did his best to distract her from the initial malaises. It is for her that he composed the first of the "cent sonnets," and it is also to her that he dedicated the entire unpublished volume. *A mon Lapin,* he ventured, a *darling* dedication which is surpassed only by the one addressed to her in *L'Ecume des Jours,* and which reads: *Pour mon Bibi.* Michelle had, of course, a likable and lovable character, as Simone de Beauvoir corroborates: "One always liked her because she never preferred herself. Gay and a little mysterious, very discreet and very present, she was always a charming companion."[8] It is interesting to note that Vian's autoportrait as it appears in the description of Baron Visi (anagram for Boris Vian) in the later novel, *Trouble dans les Andains,* is entirely different and points to a personage who is much more egocentric and more of an introvert than a good companion: "Baron Visi measured 1.87 m. He was. . .pale, and his blue eyes with the eyelids always half closed gave to everyone the impression of a profoundly cerebral attitude."

If Vian amused his wife with his literary endeavors during her pregnancy, he also left her many times in order to participate in concert tours which came about as a result of his joining the Claude Abadie jazz orchestra. Thus, his literary beginnings and those of music intermingle. At the same time, too, he continued his studies at the Ecole Centrale until a few months after the birth of his son, at which time he received his engineering diploma.

Soon thereafter he does what his father had consistently refused to do, namely he takes on a steady job as engineer for the Association Française de Normalisation. It is for this firm that he is going to work until 1946. Having established thus a certain amount of financial security for himself and for his family, which also involved permanent residence in Paris, he is now free to devote his leisure time to literature. In fact, immediately after his employment, in early 1943, he begins to write *Trouble dans les Andains* and *Vercoquin et le plancton.* At the same time he publishes poems for the *Bulletin* of the Hot Club of France under the pseudonym of Bison Ravi. Later, in the period 1944-45, following the liberation of Paris, Vian has numerous contacts with American soldiers and even participates as trumpet player in a jazz orchestra of the Special Service. Paralleling these musical activities are his continued attempts at literature, especially the short stories of the later *Les Fourmis* and the chronicles which he writes under the pen name of Hugo Hachebuisson for a periodical called *Les Amis des Arts.* During the same period, like most young intellectuals at the time, he becomes acquainted with and has a certain penchant for the Existentialism of Sartre. In fact, in the beginning of 1946 he makes the personal acquaintance of Sartre and of Simone de Beauvoir.

Yet, if Sartre and his followers think it imperative to be *en situation,*[9] the greatest part of Vian adult life is mostly that of a spectator, objective and impartial, at least in his own mind. He could never have the discipline necessary to total *engagement.* If he stands against a number of *isms,* and if he engages in many polemics during his life, he does so in a mockish tone, laughingly and amusingly. Never does he preach, and never does he defend any position *ex cathedra.* His works are neither *romans* nor *pièces à thèse,* and he has little concern for seeing his views adopted. In fact, more often than not he refuses to take himself seriously and to admit that he has any hard-core views. In his personal life, as well as in his works, there is always a half comical, half austere tone which defies definition and categorization. Perhaps the attitude which he adopted during the war years is one which describes best his *non-engagement,* for he is not attracted either by the resistance movement, nor by the possibility of collaborating with the enemy. His rebellion against the Vichy government is simply limited to playing jazz, buying forbidden books by American authors, and participating in what was then called the Zazou movement. The zazous liked to translate, into French, American jazz compositions whose performance had been forbidden by the occuping German forces: thus the song of George Gershwin "Lady Be Good" becomes in French "Les Bigoudis;" "Tiger Rag" and "St. Louis Blues" are entitled "La Rage du Tigre," and "La Tristesse de Saint-Louis," respectively. But according to Simone de Beauvoir, Vian's activities in the Zazou movement were not limited to retitling American songs. He and his friends "organized *terrible* parties; emptied cellars full of wine and broke furniture, thus imitating warlike procedures; they dabbled in the black market, were anarchists, apolitical, against their pro-Pétain parents, and displayed a provoking Anglomania; they imitated the elegance of the English ways of eating, their accent, and in general, the manners of British snobs."[10]

More specifically, Vian's attitude during the war can be deduced from the mockery he made of Sartre's well-known argument according to which the cowardly man prefers to objectify himself rather than come to grips with decisions. Vian remarked that the ultimate way of objectifying oneself is through death. Therefore suicide must be avoided; therefore war must be avoided: "War is a social phenomenon of capital interest because all those who engage in it may earn a pure and complete objectification and thus reach the corpse state. . .but war does not provide a solution because often one is not killed."[11] He thus implies that those who choose to go to war, especially volunteers, are cowards, and unintelligent cowards at that, because if they remain alive, their efforts have been in vain. On the contrary, the one who is a conscientious objector becomes a truly courageous person, for he refuses to turn into an object.

Yet, his antimilitarism does not result only in arguments that are too subtle. In the middle 1950's, at the time of the Algerian crisis, he composed and interpreted a number of songs which drew the ire of the *anciens combattants* (war veterans), and of government censorship. His "Le Déserteur," whose public performance was forbidden at the time, became posthumously a national and international success: the Peter, Paul and Mary group performed it at numerous domestic festivals where the Vietnam war was being questioned, and in 1966, in France, it was the most popular *American import.* To the public accusation of the critic Henri Magnan that he "was spitting on tombs that were still fresh," Vian responded in *L'Equarrisage pour tous* by explaining his position regarding war as follows:

I regret to be one of those to whom war does not inspire any patriotic reflections. . .nor any murderous enthusiasm, nor any poignant, or sudden piety—it gives me nothing but a despairing anger, total, against the absurdity of battles which are word battles but which kill men of flesh. . . . War is a grotesque thing. . .and those who are amused by it believe that they are, in general, entitled to extend it so that it should incorporate those who are not amused by it. War is one of the multiple faces of intolerance, and a most destructive one. That is why, in the reduced measure in which something written, and therefore artificial, can have any effect, I have tried to react against it.

The antimilitarist that he is, Vian considers all surviving *anciens combatants* as failures of wars. On this subject he explains: "The fighter who did not get himself killed has the mentality of a failure; therefore he will do his best to compensate for his deficiency and will fall into the trap of preparing his next; or, how can he prepare it well since he just got away from the preceding one and consequently, from the point of view of war, he is disqualified."[12] It is clear, then, that the next deficiency has to be another entanglement; therefore, the only way to eliminate future wars is to get rid of those who would take part in them. It is for this reason that Vian writes a *Petit manuel d'anéantissement du militaire* which appears in the volume *Textes et Chansons* (pp. 107-16). And the same *Dossier* mentioned above contains the logical solution, a final and total war which will abolish all the future ones because no soldier will escape alive. "May I be believed: The day when no one will return from war will mark the first well-made war. On that day we shall notice that all abortive attempts which had been made at peace had been until then the work of amateurs."[13] In fact, Vian has been often tempted by definitive and total destruction as a solution to unsolvable problems, as can be seen in the dénouement of his plays and of some of his novels. This is in line, of course, with his obsession with man's disintegration due to disease and age, as well as with his constant fear of and disgust for death.

To summarize, then, Vian's *non-engagement* is revealed not only by a certain amount of Anglomania and by a tongue-in-cheek approach to such serious problems as war and patriotism, but also in his many antimilitarist writings, and especially in the very popular musical compositions which deride those who take themselves too seriously and fall into the simpleton's trap of "Work, Family, Country, and Honor to the Unknown Soldier."[14]

The only commitment to which Vian sticks almost without interruption is that to literature. In 1946 he finishes the manuscript of *L'Ecume des jours,* and during the same year he continues writing the short stories of the later *Les Fourmis,* as well as articles for Sartre's *Les Temps modernes.* In June, 1946, he becomes a candidate for the coveted Prix de la Pléiade, which goes instead to the Abbé Jean Grosjean. Vian's pride and confidence in himself are hurt, of course, but he was only twenty-six at the time, and it was indeed an honor even to be considered by the jury of the highly reputable literary prize which signifies, usually, a rather definitive literary consecration. Later, he will laugh off the incident by giving the name of Petitjean to the ridiculous priest of *L'Automne à Pékin.* As a matter of fact, the setback does not disturb him too much, for in the course of the same year, namely between the fifth and the twentieth of August, he writes the entire manuscript of *J'irai cracher sur vos tombes.* He undertook the novel as a result of a bet with his friend Jean d'Halluin who was in charge of the Editions du Scorpion, and who wanted to publish an Anglo-Saxon type thriller. The book appeared under the pseudonym of Vernon Sullivan, and the cover informs the reader that Sullivan is only the translator of the work.

J'irai cracher sur vos tombes was almost an unheard-of commercial success: in a short period of time it sold in excess of half a million copies, and it provided Vian with considerable financial security for some time to come. His good fortune, however, was soon followed by scandal. Several months later, in February, 1947, in a small hotel of Montparnasse, a young man called Edmond Rougé kills his concubine. Next to the corpse, the police find a copy of *J'irai cracher sur vos tombes* opened to the passage where the hero also kills his mistress. Vernon Sullivan is immediately described by the press as an indirect assassin, and the President of the Cartel d'Action Sociale et Morale introduces a lawsuit against the author. The case is debated in Court and in the press for a number of years, but it is only in November, 1948, that Vian admits to the judge that he is the writer of the controversial novel. In the summer of 1950 the government officially forbids further sales of the book, and in the following year Vian is sentenced for affront to public morals and has to pay a fine of one hundred thousand francs.

Spurred by the limelight cast upon him, his publications begin to proliferate. In 1947 *Vercoquin et le plancton* hits the market, and in the fall of that same year he publishes *L'Automne à Pékin* and *Les Morts ont tous la même peau.* At the same time he continues to play the trumpet for various musical groups, and to take part in many radio programs. The following year, 1948, is indeed an eventful one for him, for it sees not only the birth of his daughter, Carole, but also the publication of *Et on tuera tous les affreux* by the newspaper *France-Dimanche,* as well as the presentation of the play version of *J'irai cracher sur vos tombes.* In addition, he makes a number of controversial speeches, notably the one entitled "The usefulness of an erotic literature" at the Club Saint-James. Still in the course of 1948 he publishes *Barnum's Digest* and translates his own *J'irai cracher sur vos tombes* under the title *I shall spit on your graves.*

1949, however, marks the beginning of a number of reversals in Vian's personal life and in his career as well. To begin with, being always somewhat of a spender and a bad manager of money, he is unable to pay his taxes, and the fiscal authorities pursue him. On the domestic level, he gets along less and less well with his wife. In fact, according to her, the deterioration of their marriage goes back to 1945. The initial arguments were then prompted by financial considerations, but through the intermediary of Wolf in *L'Herbe rouge* Vian explains the underlying causes:

I got married because I physically needed a woman; because I had a certain repugnance for lying and courting, which obligated me to get married when I was too young to be able to please someone physically. Because she was a woman whom I thought I loved, and whose milieux, opinions, characteristics, were convenient. I got married almost without knowing the female sex. What was the result of all that? No passion, the slow initiation of too virgin a woman, lassitude on my part. . .precisely at the time when she began to be interested, I was too tired to make her happy; too tired because I had waited for too long the violent response for which I had hoped in spite of all logic. She was pretty. I loved her all right, I liked her. It was not sufficient.

Thus, Vian evokes through his hero, with understanding and sensitivity, the psychological and sexual reasons which were at the bottom of his conjugal problems. These problems, unoriginal of course, need not alienate his followers who surely recognize them to be at the root of many initial marital misunderstandings which lead to infidelity and divorce. The break between Boris and Michelle was not the result of petty arguments; it came about as a logically progressive building up of tensions for which no society has yet found a solution. Beset by financial difficulties and increasingly poor domestic relations, it is no wonder, then, that Vian began to look elsewhere for relaxation. At one of those open-air cocktail parties given weekly by the editor Gaston Gallimard, he makes the acquaintance of a young Swiss dancer named Ursula Kübler, who had recently moved to Paris. He manages to rent a small apartment on the Boulevard de Clichy, and lives with her for a number of years. Although his divorce from Michelle is pronounced in 1952, he will not marry his mistress until 1954.

From the point of view of his career, beginning in 1949 the reversals are patently obvious. He and his editor have to spend a great deal of time in Court, and his condemnation, later, to a heavy fine, does not help his financial security at all. Although he continues to write at a rapid pace *(L'Equarrissage pour tous, Le Dernier des métiers, L'Herbe rouge* and *Elles se rendent pas compte* are all published in 1950), sales are extremely poor and hardly sufficient to cover editorial and publishing expenses. Unsuccessful with original works, Vian turns, then, to translations. The list of authors translated 1951-53 includes such writers as Strindberg, Dorothy Baker, Ray Bradbury, A. E. Van Vogt, and General Omar Bradley. At the same time he becomes an *aficionado* of science-fiction and begins to attend the Club des Savanturiers. This is the beginning of the period in Vian's life when he no longer seems endowed with the talent to produce works of lasting literary quality. But to his detractors on this score, Vian replies later within the text of an article:

One sees from time to time benevolent advisors, fat on fat cheeses, deplore the scorn into which some writers abandon art for the low, material tasks of journalism, popular songs, novels that are not literature, or translations, that is to say for pure and simple grocery items. It is regrettable that these advisors forget an elementary truth: *primum vivere.* It is easy to create when one has the material means for living without prostituting oneself.[15]

It is apparent, then, that even in these difficult times in his career, when he had to be often a dilettante and a bohemian, he maintained nevertheless, toward himself at least, an obvious dignity and integrity. Such qualities of his character were not evident to his enemies, and were blurred even to friends. What the latter misunderstood, or envied, was Vian's marvelous ability for adaptation: that he survived by means of lyrics, journalism, translations, and science-fiction, was considered, to a greater or lesser degree, an act of treason; this, apparently, in order not to have to come to terms with the *primum vivere* truism with which

Vian wrestled. A portrait of the author (as he looked at the time) by his friend Billetdoux is significant in this context: "He has a head like a moon slice, milky and pink, a delicate mouth, a fine nose, eyes filled with limpid liquid, and a forehead like that of a newly born child. On the contrary, his extended arm and legs which abandon themselves to movement. . .his skin habitually light, in harmony with his features, his air of a hunting dog or of an animal ruminating the forests, announce his predominant quality: adaptability."[16]

Another factor which fed the scandalmongers was Vian's joining of the College of Pataphysicians in 1952. This bogus group had been formed in 1948 by a number of avant-garde writers and artists for the devout purpose of counterfeiting the pompous ceremonies, meetings, and dress of the Académie Française and other consecrated official bodies. The most important quality of the College was in fact formulated publicly by Vian, as follows: "Only the College of Pataphysicians does not undertake to save the world." His membership in it was simply another aspect of his *non-engagement,* but was also prompted by the fact that one of the group's subcommittees had seen a presentation of the play *L'Equarrissage pour tous* and had adulated publicly the author. Vian was naturally attracted by Pataphysics, which has been described as "the science beyond metaphysics," and which is akin to most of the ideas of the Surrealists, the Dadaists, and the contemporary avant-garde writers. This *science* had been introduced initially in a metaphysical farce entitled *Ubu Roi,* written by the playwright Alfred Jarry in 1896. Of course, the organization of the College of Pataphysicians appealed to Vian's sense of humor and to his need of sarcasm as a defense mechanism. This august body, with a publication of its own, *Cahiers du Collège de Pataphysique,* has an absurdly involved hierarchy of Rulers and Commissions under the supervision of a Vice-Curator, six Proveditors-General, Officials of the Rogation and Executive Organon, as well as a full Corps of Satraps. Moreover, it boasts many a renowned member, among others the film director and poet René Clair, the celebrated novelist Raymond Queneau, and the poet Jacques Prévert. Eugène Ionesco himself is one of the Satraps and the holder of the *Ordre de la Grande Gidouille* (the big belly), order whose promoter was none other than Vian himself. The mockery that the College of Pataphysicians makes of metaphysics can be seen in Ionesco's assertion: "One does not become a Pataphysician, one is a pataphysician. If you commit suicide you are a pataphysician, and if you choose not to kill yourself you are still a pataphysician."[17]

When asked about the activities of the College, he replied to the same interviewer: "The best activity is to refrain from all activity." Many of its involvements, however, were indeed to the liking of Boris Vian. For example, members would meet regularly in order to counterfeit and mock such trappings as honors, processionals, decorations, and titles. Vian was not only the promoter of the *Ordre* mentioned above, but also in charge of the Extraordinary Commission on Clothing, and a frequent contributor to the publication of the College. His activities in Pataphysics, therefore, could not help but alienate many editors, reviewers, and critics who might have been, otherwise, more lenient, if not more objective, toward his literary output. As things were, however, his last novel, published in 1953, *L'Arrache-coeur,* had only negative reviews, as did his two musical contributions of the same year, *Le Chevalier de neige,* an opera presented at the Normandy Festival of Caen, and his adaptation of Georg Kaiser's *L'Incendie de l'Opéra.*

III   *The Final Years*

Following his February, 1954, marriage to Ursula Kübler, Boris Vian pursues his musical activities more than his literary endeavors. In the course of 1954, for example, he participates in a popular song tourney throughout France, and in 1955 he tapes his many "possible" and "impossible songs." In the course of the same year he becomes the artistic director of Philips Recording Co., a job he is going to hold until 1959. In the meantime his health continues to worsen, and in July, 1956, he undergoes a crisis of pulmonary edema, which is "the result of (his) uninterrupted taxing of a heart that could hardly hold its own."[18] This crisis makes him acutely aware of impending death and, according to Arnold Kübler, he advised his wife, Ursula, "I shall not reach my fortieth birthday. . .don't depend on me too much."[19] He is obliged to remain in bed for quite some time and, on 7 September 1956, readers could see in the newspaper *L'Express* the following notice: "Just before summer vacation, the death sentence had been pronounced. Having come out miraculously from the edema crisis, Boris Vian can no longer engage in any efforts now. His doctors advise him to take it easy while waiting for the surgery techniques to improve in order to assure to him a normal existence." And the article went on to quote the public declaration of the patient: "If there are twenty chances out of a hundred that an operation be successful, I want to try it, for better to die than to molder in this fashion."[20] 'The operation never took place, however. Instead, he was put on daily medicine, and in 1957 he suffered another edema. Nevertheless, he continued to write: *Les*

Bâtisseurs d'Empire, and numberless articles for *Jazz-Hot* where, interestingly, he makes frequent allusions to his disease and mentions how he even has trouble holding on to his pen, and how he can hear the palpitations of his heart which make his chest vibrate and which are a constant, auditive reminder, for the others, of his physical insufficiency.

Rest, however, would only constitute capitulation, and the only thing he can do against the disease is to keep as active as possible. It is thus that in 1958 he puts the finishing touches on the opera *Fiesta* which he writes in cooperation with Darius Milhaud, a work whose première takes place in Berlin. He makes speeches here and there, continues to write articles, becomes involved in heated arguments with the director of the film version of *J'irai cracher sur vos tombes* and, in 1959, he even manages to obtain the role of Prévent in the scandalous film *Les Liaisons dangereuses.* In the course of the same year he switches from Philips to the Barclay Recording Co., in the same capacity of artistic director. On 23 June, in the morning, Vian has an appointment at the movie studio where he is scheduled to view part of the film version of *J'irai cracher sur vos tombes* in order to determine whether or not he can lend his support to the project. After ten minutes of attendance, seated in an armchair, his diseased heart distorted by the edema, he collapses and dies. The funeral takes place the same day at Ville-d'Avray.

It is then that the posthumous life of Boris Vian begins. After his death, and still in 1959, his *Bâtisseurs d'Empire* enjoys an enormous stage success, and the Association of Friends of Boris Vian is formed. The group numbers many famous persons: Maurice Béjart, Aimé Césaire, René Clair, Jacques Delerue, Max Ernst, Arnold Kübler, Michel Leiris, Baron Jean Mollet, the Préverts, Darius Milhaud, and Jean-Paul Sartre, to mention only a few. The critic Pierre Kast commented on the author's short life as follows: "Lucidity, justice of the heart and of reasoning, a penchant for friendship and brotherhood, an absolute lack of selfishness, and a formidable impatience to wear out the multiple talents given to him by a host of gods, have been incarnated in the course of his short and dense existence whose qualities we are just beginning to uncover."[21] The same critic wrote, three years after Vian's death, in the preface of a new edition of *L'Herbe rouge:* "The tumultuous and diverse life of Boris Vian was in the image of the possibilities, of the probabilities, and of the contradictions of today's world. As one used to say about Gide that he was a contemporary par excellence, I feel like saying that Boris Vian is the contemporary par excellence."[22]

However, Vian's posthumous popularity need not blind one to that which he enjoyed in his life. Although, often, one could not find his novels on the shelves of the best Parisian bookstores, on the Rive Gauche, where one browses more than one buys, he was nevertheless, and for a long time, a topic of conversation of the literary elite. Vian's modernity and present vogue reside in the fact that many of the activities in which he enjoyed becoming involved, science-fiction, jazz, "nonsense" literature, the absurd, have, since his death, become established and uncontested cultural endeavors. While he appealed, during his life, only to an embryonic and anticipatory public, after his death he was looked upon as a precursor, indeed as a *seer*. "Vian, misunderstood just as Stendhal was in the course of his life, adorned as Lautréamont, by the aureola of a precocious death, a multifarious genius like certain Surrealists, had to take his place in the heart and spirit of the new generation."[23] Indeed, his tastes, his choices, his enthusiasm, corresponded with and responded to those of the generation born or raised around the second half of the twentieth century. His life was the object of adulation and scorn; his career as a writer and composer gave rise to equally contradictory reactions. Above all, his death, medically foreseen, scientifically delayed, romantically awaited with a mixture of fear and dare, emulated the way that the public had come to expect writers of repute to die: abruptly, as Roger Nimier in his sports car, as Albert Camus, on the road, at high speed, a year later, all supplying, even in their terminal agonal spasms, the material for a *fait divers* newspaper item.

In 1959, the otherwise eminent Yale professor and critic Henri Peyre introduced Boris Vian to his students as follows: "He is one of the numerous *enfants terribles* of French Existentialism...he may be amusing, spiritual and funny, although never solid nor convincing."[24] But, as the following pages will attempt to demonstrate, the literary heritage left by Boris Vian, unlike his death and many events in the course of his life, surpasses the temporariness of a *fait divers,* and goes beyond it, propelling the author into a persuasive and permanent position among the better exponents of French letters in the twentieth century.

CHAPTER 2

The Novels

I   J'irai cracher sur vos tombes

A first novel is not usually a success, it is not supposed to be a success, and when it is, it often annoys and upsets the majority of critics, to say nothing of the spiteful attitude to which it gives rise in more established writers. That Vian, an unknown, managed (a) to sell some half a million copies in a short period of time and (b) to get himself sued, were considered feats of rare audacity which kindled the enmity of many, and maintained it alive for most until after his death, when the author began to be known not only for his exploration of eroticism in *J'irai cracher sur vos tombes* but, also, for works of more intrinsic literary value.

The story of the genesis of Vian's first publication is perhaps more interesting than the novel itself. In August, 1946, Vian was on vacation at Saint-Jean-de-Monts in the Vendée. With him and his wife was also Georges d'Halluin, a friend and fellow musician in the Claude Abadie orchestra, and also brother of Jean d'Halluin, director of the Editions du Scorpion. The latter's company was in deep financial trouble and needed a best seller for survival. What the editor had in mind, specifically, was an American-type novel of the kind in vogue in Europe at the end of World War II; that is, one containing the proper amounts of adventure, drunkenness, brutality, sexual aggressiveness and social considerations, hiding, but obscuring only poorly, the most desolate loneliness and boredom, sadness and sadism. Boris is reported to have replied to his friend's brother: "A best seller? Give me ten days and I shall manufacture one for you."[1] His wife, Michelle, launched an encouragement and a dare by saying: "Go ahead, Boris, make him a best seller!"[2] What followed was a bet between Vian and Jean d'Halluin, the terms of which specified that the former obligated himself to write, in a matter of days, what would become a successful American-type thriller. More importantly, the bet was between Vian the potential and Vian the actual author, for although he had tried his hand at various kinds of compositions for a number of years, he had not published anything of consequence. The writing of *J'irai cracher sur vos tombes* became, thus, a kind of *tour de force,* the subject of which had to be something readily available and à la mode.

Of course, in 1946, French liberals were becoming increasingly intrigued by the racial problems in the United States. Several articles on the subject had appeared in Sartre's *Les Temps modernes,* and in the summer of the same year many French newspapers had devoted columns to the lynchings taking place in a number of Southern states. The aversion of French intellectuals was focused on Sartre's *La Putain respectueuse,* an extremely popular play which attacked the status of race relations in America. In addition, the American magazine *Collier's,* to which Vian used to subscribe, in its 3 August issue carried an article entitled "Who is a Negro?" which pointed to the fact that over two million American Negroes had crossed the color line and were becoming racially unrecognizable. With the above as a background, the author chose as his hero Lee Anderson, a young man who looks like a White and lives among the Whites. After his brother was lynched for having lived with a white woman, Lee decides to seek vengeance and moves to a small Southern town where he soon meets two young girls, Jean and Lou Asquith, who belong to one of the best resident families. He seduces and makes Jean pregnant, pursues Lou as well, and finally kidnaps both sisters while promising to marry each, although in reality he plots to kill them both. Lou refuses at first to give herself to him and, in the ensuing struggle, Lee Anderson's arm is injured. Enraged by the sight of blood, he advances the previously foreseen murder time, and butchers the body of Lou. Jean, on the other hand, allows herself to be strangled without posing the least resistance. In the end, following a cinematographic pursuit, replete with blood and destruction, Lee is killed by the police and his body is nevertheless hanged by the town's people, "because he was a Negro."

Of course, Vian was not an *engagé,* and *J'irai cracher sur vos tombes* was not written primarily for the purpose of defending the American Black. The author was sincere, however, when he attacked racial segregation in America, especially since he had always sympathized with the feelings of so many great jazz players who found consistently more freedom of movement and greater appreciation in France than in the United States. Also, throughout the years, he had written in

Jazz-Hot many articles attesting to the contributions to music of American Negroes. Nevertheless, for Vian, any skin color was a mask, and racial difficulties constituted only one aspect of the unsolvable problem of man's alienation from man.

Nor was Vian concerned in the present novel with the glorification of eroticism. In fact, *J'irai cracher sur vos tombes* never obtained the success of an *Histoire d'O*,[3] for example, nor was it a purely pornographic work. While the variety of sexual experiences described is almost unlimited, there is a gradation and a rhythm which betray the accomplished writer who, although unpublished until then, possessed nevertheless the required talent and technique. Vian does not fall into the trap of monotony and repetition, shortcomings which usually underscore pornographic books. He makes extensive use of brevity and allusions even when he appears to be otherwise quite explicit, in order to maintain interest and suspense. That is why it is important not to take too seriously Vian's own comments concerning his novel: "A book which, literarily speaking, doesn't deserve much attention at all."[4]

On the contrary, if we accept at their face value Vian's two aims in composing *J'irai cracher sur vos tombes,* namely to prove that (a) he could write and (b) he could make money writing, the enterprise was eminently successful. In spite of the novel's subject and character, and in spite of the traditionally reluctant attitude of critics in even acknowledging works that border on the pornographic (especially at a time when patriotism and the dignity of a France victorious and free were flung before the face of a public still high, in 1946, on its miraculous survival[5]), *J'irai cracher sur vos tombes* elicited, nevertheless, a number of neutral and mildly favorable comments which went unnoticed in the midst of the emotionally charged derogatory criticism which otherwise welcomed it. In the magazine *Esprit,* for example, it was labeled "a small success."[6] In *Paris-Normandie,* the reviewer of the play version lauded "the social and ethnic drama"[7] of Vian. *Paru* noted the fact that the libidinous part of the work is relegated to a minor position by comparison with the part discussing racial problems in America.[8] The reputable Jacques Lemarchand himself, who liked Vian and the play version of the novel, but could not afford to alienate the readers of *Combat* nor his friends at the Ministry of Interior, chose to review *J'irai cracher sur vos tombes* in a highly sarcastic, though not a pejorative tone:

I know well Vernon Sullivan, the author of *J'irai cracher sur vos tombes.* We met once at Columbia University, in our junior year as

Be-bops. We would cut classes in order to go read Racine in the toilet. . . . It was at that time that Vernon Sullivan came up with a curious, ingenious and very seductive theory. He had studied closely the rapports between Negroes and Whites. . . . Then life separated us until the day when I learned that he had assigned to Boris Vian, my friend and colleague, the job of spreading his thought throughout Europe. . . . Boris Vian went to work immediately. At first he gave us the translation of *J'irai cracher sur vos tombes*. One is familiar with the success that the book had. The conscience of the French was finally touched by the problem of slavery. . .the message of Vernon Sullivan reached its destination, and France, troubled, became involved in a good cause. There remained to reach the masses. . .braving nasty persecutions. . .he wrote the play currently given at Théâtre Verlaine. . .it is a show which is extremely well played. And convincing.[9]

Thus, those who did not condemn Vian for his extreme sense of commercialism, and his book *a priori* therefore, saw a number of qualities which take *J'irai cracher sur vos tombes* out of the realm of the sensational novel and into that of social and literary concern. This is not to say that the composition is devoid of certain shortcomings. For example, while the rest of the novel is written in the first person, the last three chapters are told in the third, a technical error which hurts the unity of the book, but which Vian could ill avoid because he had to describe objectively the final death scene of the narrator. The conclusion itself, Negro-martyr (Lee Anderson's body is hanged nevertheless "because he was a Negro"), is false and a bit hypocritical for Vian's own intelligence certainly precludes such an exaggeration. Another minor defect, betraying the author's lack of knowledge about this country, is evident in one of the initial pages when Lee closes the bookstore where he works by pulling down the iron shutters, an inexistent practice here, but one encountered widely on the Continent.

The question of the sincerity of the book's prefatory remarks is also one that the critics raised. To begin with, Vian was accused of lying when he affirmed that the novel's authorship belonged to Vernon Sullivan (pseudonym suggested to him by the name of a fellow musician in the Claude Abadie orchestra, Paul Vernon, and by Joe Sullivan, celebrated jazz pianist). Secondly, they imputed to him the fact that the novel was billed as "the first book of a young author whom no American editor dared to publish, denouncing in pages of an unheard violence, and whose style is equal to that of great predecessors such as Caldwell, Faulkner and Cain, the unjust suspicion to which the

Blacks are relegated in certain parts of the United States." Finally, objection was raised against the description of Vernon Sullivan: "One of these Blacks" whose story "was born out of the racial misunderstandings which are at the origin of recent lynchings, in order, once more, to call to the attention of the civilized world" the horrors which were taking place in America. However, such exaggerations were simply gobbled up by the French public of the late 1940's and, at the worst, Vian is only guilty of commercializing them. In fact, the well-known critic Robert Kanters wrote on the occasion of the publication of *J'irai cracher sur vos tombes* that "in today's style, just about anything is translated, as if the mention *translated from American* were a mark of magic fiber."[10] To the accusation that he hid under the name of the nonexistent Vernon Sullivan whose work he professed only to have translated, Boris Vian responded effectively in a letter he addressed to the newspaper *Paris-Presse:* "The procedure used. . .is not new. I have heard of a certain Mérimée, of a certain Mac Pherson, and of a certain Pierre Louys; I don't see why the superior quality of their works should justify more than in my modest case a simple and identical procedure which had nothing to do with anything crooked, but which is rather an (accepted) game."[11]

The above polemics notwithstanding, later critics, less prone to pettiness because they were more removed in time, bestowed a number of laudatory remarks on *J'irai cracher sur vos tombes.* Freddy de Vrée, for example, aptly pointed to the fact that Vian's manipulation of eroticism does not lead him to the over-use of crude terms in the present novel; on the contrary, he uses them only in jokes, "and it is this, his pudicity, it is surely there, this pudicity, a pearl and a flower, just as a nervous fear which kills but is projected into sexuality."[12] He also points to the fact that there is no scatology in *J'irai cracher sur vos tombes* and that, as Vian himself wrote in the preface to the novel, "The book is, in any case, less dirty than the Bible." It is noteworthy that in the same context the author had added: "(This is) a good theme, which, well treated, could have become a good novel, but with the risks of mediocre sales which accompany any good book; and which, treated commercially, as it was, wound up being a popular novel, one which makes for easy reading and for good sales." It is thus obvious that little quarrel can be found with Vian's lucidity. His predominant aims, those of writing and of writing for money, were eminently attained, but had nothing to do with any inherent taste for pornography. Such a judgment is indeed corroborated by his opposition to the manner in which the film version was handled.

As early as 1948 Vian had begun to work at the scenario adaptation of the novel. His friend, Jacques Dopagne, helped him in the initial efforts, but it was mostly Boris who insisted that the film treatment of the story had to undergo extensive changes. There were many reasons for his views on what the film should be like: the generally inimical press reception of *J'irai cracher sur vos tombes,* especially after the novel was linked to an actual murder,[13] the vicissitudes of the lawsuit against him; and the difficulties which he had in conjunction with some of his more controversial lyrics, to mention only a few. But above all, it was Vian's own intergrity which prompted him to seek numerous alterations for the screen version. In his unpublished correspondence with prospective producers, he wrote how inappropriate and deplorable it would be if the film were to become a vulgar study of sexuality and sadism which would be forbidden to anyone under eighteen years of age. In addition, a number of external circumstances came into play: the era of McCarthyism in the United States, the war in Algeria, and in general the racial struggles among peoples of all colors and shades of colors throughout the world. Vian wished to eliminate anything which might appear propagandistic or simplistic and, above all, he wished to soften most of the physical details that could tend to detract from a purely artistic work. In this context, Raymond Queneau wrote the following in his preface to *L'Arrache-coeur:* "Boris Vian is going to become Boris Vian."

Queneau, who was familiar with his friend's efforts, and who endorsed the projected purification of *J'irai cracher sur vos tombes,* had no way of knowing, in 1953, that producers and directors, who knew they held the rights to a potential fortune-making film, would oppose considerable resistance to any attempts at dilution of what was coarse and crass in the novel. In fact, they rejected repeatedly Vian's various versions of the scenario, and even threatened to employ their own writers who would then adapt the book as they saw fit. Under the circumstances, the only thing that Boris could do was to keep his name out of the picture. This was, almost to the end, his intention. But, as it is now known, in 1959 he was persuaded to reconsider the matter and it can be said that the movie version of *J'irai cracher sur vos tombes* precipitated the author's death not only because on the morning when he went to view it he had forgotten to take his daily medicine, but because for years the controversy had cost him numberless efforts and had simply worn him out. As Noël Arnaud wrote later: "At the moment of truth, Vernon Sullivan will not let Boris Vian possess his *J'irai cracher sur vos tombes* (rather) he will hand the work over to prowling profiteers, just as he will hand over to them his (very) life."[14]

II Vercoquin et le plancton

Vian began writing the first novel to appear under his own name in 1943, managed to get it accepted by Gaillimard in 1945, but will not have it published until two years later, after considerable reworking of the text. In the manuscript of "Elements of a Biography (Without Interest)" the author gave the following information concerning the book:

In 43 wrote a novel especially in order to show to the zazous, *aficionados* of bad jazz and bad *surprise-parties,* how things were in the good old days (35 to 39). Called it *Vercoquin et le plancton,* which also contains an attempt to describe what office life is like.
For a long time very close to Jean Rostand and his son, Francois, finding novel funny, has Queneau read it. Approval with certain reservations by the latter. Reworked text accepted by Gallimard.

Jean Rostand, the famous biologist, as well as his son, were residents of Ville-d'Avray and friends of the Vian family. In fact, François appears in the novel under the name of Corneille Monprince (Monprince was François' real nickname). Later, during the quarrel engendered by *J'irai cracher sur vos tombes,* Jean Rostand broke with the Vians and, after the author's death, he refused to join the *Club des Amis de Boris Vian.*

The cover of *Vercoquin et le plancton* sets the tone for the entire text. It depicts a cartoon of the author in a prisoner's garb, complete with number stamped on his chest, and base of a vase instead of legs standing on a three-legged stool. The caption reads: *"Vercoquin et le plancton* by Reverend Boris Vian of the Compagnie de Jésus, with a portrait of the author by his aunt Josée de Zamora." The book contains a *prélude* in which the novelist writes: *"Vercoquin* is not a Realist novel in the sense that all that is told herein has taken place indeed." And then, ironically, he goes on to explain:

When you have spent your youth picking up cigarette butts at Deux-Magots,[15] washing dishes in a somber and filthy backroom, covering yourself, in winter, with old newspapers, in order to keep warm on the icy bench which was at the same time your bedroom, your home and your bed, when you wound up being carried to the police station by two cops for having stolen bread from a bakery store (not knowing yet that it is much easier to rob it from the shopping bag of a housewife returning from the market); when you have lived from day to day 365 1/4 days a year like the colibri on the branch of the *micocoulier,* [16] in a word when you have fed yourself on garbage, you have the title of Realist novelist, and the people who read you think to themselves: this man has lived what he narrates, has felt what he depicts. . . . But I have slept always in a good bed, I don't like to smoke, garbage doesn't tempt me at all, and had I stolen anything, it would have been meat.

Thus, like the Realist author he might have been but isn't, *Vercoquin et le plancton* is a real story that could have been fiction but isn't; at any rate, it is not entirely fictitious.

The main character of the narration is Le Major. He is a zazou who, like Rabelais' Panurge in the third book, wonders whether or not he should marry. At a *surprise-partie* of the type that the author attended and organized innumerable times before and during the war years, he meets Zizanie who becomes, like Don Quixote's Dulcinea, the hero's object of blind love. But Le Major has a rival, Antioche, and because he is also an alleged friend he tells the hero as soon as he sees the girl: "Listen. I am not going to let you make a blunder. I am going to take care of her a little today, and then I'll tell you if she's good enough for you or not." He does, and the experience not having been too bad, Antioche is going to help Le Major get ready for marriage by finding him a steady employment. Through traffic of influence he obtains for him a position with the Consortium National de l'Unification Léon-Charles Miqueut (a mock firm standing for AFNOR where Vian in fact worked), and his job is going to be that of streamlining *surprise-parties.* After a number of adventures, funny, incredible, engaging and gigantic in proportions, the marriage between Le Major and Zizanie takes place in the course of a final *suprise-partie* which is both a ludicrous and unexpected apotheosis: little by little, as the guests partake of the interminable buffet and assault each other verbally and physically, explosions occur, feeding on each other until no one escapes, except Le Major and Antioche. Perplexed, the former wonders now if he is the marrying kind or not.

It is clear, then, that *Vercoquin et le plancton* is the novel of a youth, for the youth—that is, for the young of all ages. After its publication Vian became known as the "spiritual Pope of the Bobby-soxers,"[17] but the title is not entirely indicative of the author's all-encompassing intentions. For what he attempted to do was not merely to describe the limitless world of carefree pleasures to which the young abandon themselves blindly, but also the dangers to which such abandonment exposes them. After all, with the exception of two, all characters perish in their self-destructive glorification of the senses. But he did not wish to spare the older generations: those who move within the confining, restrictive and constrictive world of balance sheets and machines, the AFNOR universe he knew so well, that of standardization, where laborious activity is equated with the nonhuman activity of the *nothons* (word he invents and which probably derives from the English *nothing,* denoting those who are very busy and very proud to engage in meaningless tasks).

In order to accomplish his first aim, he selected as the paradigm of the pleasure-seeking youth Le Major, a friend and fellow organizer of *surprise-parties,* whom he had met first at Cap-Breton in 1940. His real name was Jacques Loustalot, son of the mayor of Saint-Martin-de-Seignanx, a neighboring town. He was only fifteen when he and Vian met, seemed at least five years older, and acted it too. He smoked a great deal, loved jazz and jitterbug, drank copiously, and behaved in all sorts of unusual ways. At the end of World War II, for example, at one point he bought a G.I. uniform from a drunken American soldier, put it on, and went to inspect the American troops stationed at Côte d'Argent. Because he had one glass eye, often, at *surprise-parties,* he would make it come out with an adroit movement of the index finger in order to scare the female participants, or else he would swallow it in full view of everyone. The fact that, playing in this fashion he would lose it on many occasions, and that a new eye cost fifteen hundred francs, did not bother him at all. After the war, tells Claude Léon, a friend of both Le Major and Vian,

there was a great vogue of going to *surprise-parties* where one was not invited. To *surprise-parties* with live music, as we furnished the music, we were invited. But there were others, without orchestra, *surprise-parties* where they used a record player. Le Major would show up and, naturally, they wanted to throw him out. Then, in revenge, he would launch himself on the record player, would grab the box of needles (it was still the time of phonograph needles) and swallow it without hesitation. And in the evening, or next day, or several days later, one would see needles coming out from all the joints of Le Major.[18]

His frequent exits from parties through a window, or by climbing to the top of the building and letting himself down on a staircase made with the hostess' sheets, always intrigued the audience and endeared him to many, for one never knew what to expect of him. In addition, he boasted often that at age ten he had attempted to commit suicide, but that all he had managed to accomplish was to lose an eye. In fact, he would always speak of suicide as of an undertaking that is not any more idiotic than any other. Actually, he died under mysterious circumstances in 1948, and neither friends nor authorities could determine if the fall was deliberate, or the accidental result of still another one of his flying exits.

Vian admired and loved Le Major. He was, for him, a prototype, the incarnation of a *style of life,* a person who flees from the world of patterns and balance, from compromises and "honest" corruption, from numbers and computers, in order to seek refuge in one where words and anecdotes reign supreme. In such a world people are rich, lazy, and sensuous; but also intelligent and sensitive. They are a mixed bunch of prostitutes and drunkards, but they are also real (if sometimes phony) musicians and artists. They get caught in the questionable but luminous aura of a vertigo which is both plausible and impossible and which, whether ending in facile joy or permanent disaster, has contributed to a fuller existence. *Vercoquin et le plancton,* just as *Trouble dans les Andains*[19] (written before but published much later), in which Le Major also appears, is a chronicler's account of such an existence, and all the incidents narrated therein are real in the sense that they all occurred, only to a lesser degree, to the main character.

Vian's role as a rapporteur is enhanced by his typically Rabelaisian quality of looking beyond the corny and the coarse, to what his predecessor called *la substantifique moelle:*[20] the idea behind the insulting word, the revolt hidden in excesses, the often deep meaning under the recesses of the *acte gratuit.* And all this he is able to do, like Rabelais, while being exceedingly amusing.

His humor is first apparent in his choice of names of various characters. Antioche, recalling the name of a number of Greek gods, and Zizanie, which figuratively means discord, have been mentioned already. But there are also Professor Epaminondas Lavertu, Member of the Institute, and "famous throughout the world for his work concerning the influence of Saturday night alcoholism on the reproductive functions of mechanical workers," the chief engineer Toucheboeuf, whose name is self-explanatory, Emmanuel Pigeon who kills a giraffe by combing it excessively, and others. These personages and their names, as well as a number of repeatedly used archaisms *(donzelle, compaigns, huis, embesteurs)*[21]; smack more of allegorical persons and terms in vogue in the literature of the sixteenth century rather than in that of the sixteenth *arrondissement.*

His humor consists also in narrating everything as if language does not have to conform to reality, but reality to language which, in this fashion, creates its own universe. This is a procedure that antinovelists and antidramatists will employ consistently in the 1950's and the 1960's, one that reveals Vian as a precursor of more famous verbal magicians such as Ionesco and Beckett, or most of his fellow Satraps at the College of Pataphysicians. Of course, his linguistic virtuosity can be appreciated best only in the original French text, for very little would come through in translation. Nevertheless, at least one illustration appears in order, and the first page of the novel might serve the purpose:

Since he wanted to do things correctly, Le Major decided that his adventures would begin this time at the precise moment when he would meet Zizanie. The weather was splendid. The garden was decorating itself with flowers that had just bloomed, whose roots formed, on the paths, a carpet cracking under one's feet. A gigantic tropical menu covered with its shadow the angle formed by the place where met the northern and southern walls of the sumptuous park which surrounded the house, one of the many houses of Le Major. It is in this intimate atmosphere, to the chant of the secular dove, that, in the morning, Antioche Tambrétambre, Le Major's right arm, has installed the bench of arbuscle wood painted green, which one used in such occasions. And what was the occasion? It is now time to say it: it was February, in full summer heat, and Le Major was going to be twenty-one years old. So, he was giving a *surprise-partie* at his home in Ville d'Avrille.

In these two paragraphs, as in most of the pages which follow, logic is only apparent, and words, instead of naming things and situations, give birth to their own reality like malignant cells that divide and multiply outside of reason. Why does he want "to do things correctly?" Why "this time?" How does Le Major know that he is going to meet Zizanie? Why is the dove "secular?" How can northern and southern walls meet? How is it that we are in full summer heat in the month of February? There are no answers to these questions, and in fact it is important that there not be any. What matters, and what appeals to the reader, is that words, and combinations of words, are endowed with their own life and humor, without necessarily describing real and comical events outside. These, to cause laughter, need language as a vehicle to translate (and, therefore, possibly to betray) and bring to the reader whatever intrinsic humoristic possibilities they possess. On the contrary, words, when used as Vian does, need not translate, nor transport comical elements; rather they expose the reader immediately and directly to the laughter-causing ingredients which are part of their very own fabric. Thus, the life of characters is complemented, in *Vercoquin et le plancton* and in books like it, by the life of the language which they use, and which the author uses in relation to them. A dual humanity emerges, that of heroes and heroines, and that of the words through which we meet them, providing, therefore, a kind of super-reality, the very one to which pataphysicians, within and in spite of their incongruous rites and ceremonies, aspire most devoutly.

In this super-reality things and animals are capable of human feelings and reactions, and the results are not only humorous, but intellectually intriguing. For example, speaking of records, Vian writes: "(they were waiting), full of indifference, for the moment when, tearing their skin with its sharp caress, the needle of the record-player would snatch from their spiraled soul the clamor imprisoned at the very bottom of their black grooves." When the hero opens a door unexpectedly and discovers a copulating couple, "a swear word, which had been waiting for a long time, greeted the appearance of Le Major and left the room with him, carefully closing the door." Or consider the following description of a mackintosh which, "domesticated, wearing a red belt, was taking a walk through the paths, with a melancholic air, regretting its native hills where the bagpiper grew," and which "upon hearing Le Major's bird call, licked his hand, jumped twelve feet high and moved off, saying, 'Pssh!' " In fact, both the flora and the fauna of *Vercoquin et le plancton* are unusual, complementing all that is odd in the humans who populate the novel.

The men and women of the narrative appear to be moved by a spirit of camaraderie only, not by any notion of what is right or wrong. Le Major likes everyone, and everyone is attracted by his gentleness, his savoir-faire, his friendship and easy-going manner. Actually, the latter are values which are dearest to Vian, for they, above all, engender and maintain strong rapports between *copains*.[22] In this world of friends, male friends, females play a secondary and accessory role. They are rarely bright (at a *surprise-partie,* one of the protagonists counsels: "Don't try to appear intelligent. They never understand. Those who understand are already married."), are seen infrequently in a vertical position, and only serve the pleasure of oversexed young men who objectify them very matter-of-factly and without the least male chauvinistic forethoughts. Actually, none of the characters is mean, least of all Le Major. They all love to eat, to drink and dance, to sleep with the opposite sex (which need not be opposite at all times) and, in the circles within which they move, they don't really hurt anyone except, through the fatigue of excesses, themselves. They are all carefree, they all abhor servitude, authority, morality, anything or anyone that could stand against the *naturel* in them.

This brings us to a consideration of Vian's second aim in writing *Vercoquin et le plancton,* namely, that of pointing to the mechanical world of the person-robot who is devoid of *naturel*. To accomplish this purpose, he takes us into the universe of the Consortium. Here, as within the confines of AFNOR, there are plans and projects, studies and standardizations, and norms which conceal abnormalities. Like any big firm, the Consortium is concerned with the process of streamlining: streamlining everything, that is, even *surprise-parties* which, by definition, ought to be run according to chance. Le Major's main assignment is precisely that of drawing a chart to be followed by those desirous of organizing *surprise-parties.* Because of its length, only part of it will be quoted here, that dealing with the procedures to be used in appropriating for oneself, in the course of the festivities, a girl who has arrived with someone else or who is occupied with another man.

If the party takes place at your house. Fix it so as to get rid of the importuner by using methods which vary according to his intrinsic nature, but by forcing yourself to remain on good terms with him. . .and by taking care to (a) prevent his partner, whom you desire, to drink too much and (b) not to drink as much as he.

Have him drink a mixture of residues susceptible to cause to turn to pink salmon an adult Senegalese. As soon as he sees less clearly, color them [the residues] with red port, and add cigarette ashes. Make him vomit:

a. Either in a sink if he only drank;
b. Or in the toilet if he ate pastries;
c. Or outside. . .if it rains.

Be sure to have his partner accompany him. Perhaps she will end up being disgusted.

Two new variants are then at one's disposal: (a) his girlfriend lets him sleep. Then you have won. (b) She is tenaciously true to him and remains with him. They are probably fiancés. Another possibility: the old fellow just won't become drunk. No solution, unless you are indeed stronger than he is.

If the party takes place at someone else's house. (a) At the house belonging to the individual whose girl you desire. He has indeed a

strong position for it is improbable that he will drink himself to sleep.
Attempt to eliminate him by one of the following methods:
1. By causing in his bathroom a well-planned flood.
I. With a piece of bicycle tube.
II. With a piece of tire.
III. By sticking an obstruction under one of the faucets of the bathtub.
2. By stuffing the toilet with two rolled newspapers (gives excellent results).
3. By causing to drink to sleep an intimate friend of the host.
(b) At anyone's house. There you are more or less of equal strength, that is to say that neither one of you has too much of a chance. Try, nevertheless, to blacken his character.

It is clear from the above that the advice given is less prone to reach the stated results than to point to the futility of detailed plans, of streamlining procedures, of methods and devices designed by such firms as AFNOR in order to delude the public into thinking that everything (and everyone) can be reduced to numbers and letters in an outline. What is not nearly so clear is Vian's biting sarcasm which becomes almost lost in translation. The dehumanized employees who people the Consortium are precisely those who, in post-war France, contributed to the economic expansion and industrialization of the country, and who gave rise to a new mass of proud workers and capitalists whose roots in the past (in the "good old days" of the past) were violently broken. But if Vian has fun in denouncing, he is also serious, and he proves himself eminently capable to anticipate concerns which will become prevalent throughout the world only in the late 1960's and the 1970's: namely, those of the antibusiness, anti-industry conservationist groups for whom progress is often a dirty word.

At the time of its publication, *Vercoquin et le plancton* received little critical adulation. Robert Kanters, for example, remarked: "The first part. . .is very funny. . .the rest is much less good, unfortunately. The satire of futile administrative complications has been done a hundred times in more amusing ways."[23] On the contrary, Jean Blanzat noted: "If there were nothing in *Vercoquin et le plancton* except the first sixty pages and the last fifty, the book would not be worth much. But there are also the personage of Miqueut and the Administration who fabricate the *nothons.*"[24] The anonymous critic of *Lettres Françaises* stated tersely: "Boris Vian goes through all sorts of contortions in order to obtain the nauseating smiles of little old senile men."[25] However, the prestigious Etienne Lalou opined that the story was "a healthy reaction against the novelists who take themselves seriously, and against Existentialism,"[26] and Aimé Patry anticipated subsequent, more appreciative criticism, when he wrote: "This novel. . .which is not to be placed in everybody's hands, shows to us an author who possesses a certain vocation of literary clown. . . . Without doubt, it will give rise, later, to a serious study on the rapports between Zazouism and Existentialism. . . . The reader who is simple-minded will undoubtedly think that it is an *idiotic* narration, but it is clear that such an appreciation is aimed at by Mr. Boris Vian."[27]

For those who reread the book after the death of the author, *Vercoquin et le plancton* revealed both the writer's talent as a chronicler, and as a foreteller of later reactions against commercialism and Existentialism. This is in general the opinion of Jacques Duchateau, for whom the literary and social validity of the novel are beyond question.[28] Freddy de Vrée, concerned more with the tone of the work than with its contents, finds that "it is an amusing narration. A good story full of humor, of life, of joy, of irony. . .the book of a young man of luxury and certitude, written by an author who enjoyed writing it" and, emulating the tone of his deceased friend, he pursues: "It doesn't harm anybody."[29] Of course, *Vercoquin et le plancton* not only does not harm anybody but, as David Noakes affirms, "it is a surprisingly good synthesis of the world of the Zazous and that of business, all the more so since Vian wrote it when he was only twenty-three years old."[30] Indeed, the novelist must have possessed a great deal of technical ability in order to be able to point, with equal humor, to the shortcomings of both worlds, and to the fact that neither could lead to lasting happiness. For happiness, whether pursued by the young through a *chasse au plaisir,* or sought by the less human ways of the Consortium, is equally elusive, if not altogether unattainable. Vian's *élan vital,* marred by heart disease and impending death, could not help but end in a pessimistic outlook. As will be shown below, such a perspective reappears in the other novels published in 1947.

III   L'Automne à Pékin

Although his original intention was to use the pseudonym Bison Ravi (the typed manuscript of the novel, now in the possession of his first wife, bears this signature), *L'Automne à Pékin* was published, in 1947, under the author's own name. The first edition was soundly unsuccessful (this, in spite of the fact that Vian, as usual, kept in mind the commercial side of the publication by devising two separate covers:

one which read, "not destined to see the light of day;" and another whose text was to be printed upside down), although in the bibliography of the later *L'Herbe rouge* it was listed as *épuisé*. Nevertheless, in subsequent years, the narrative proved to be one of those works on which editors wished to capitalize through the printing of new editions. One appeared while Vian was still alive, in 1956, bearing only some grammatical corrections and very few variants; two others appeared in 1964, and still another in 1968, all selling an increasing number of copies. As in the case of the previously discussed novel, *L'Automne à Pékin* was written, as was Vian's habit, in a hurry, yet the initial reader's reaction is one which tends to overlook the stylistic shortcomings in favor of the contaminating gall and gusto of a writer whose exuberance and exacerbation are indeed extraordinary.

Michelle, who was the first reader of the manuscript, opined, "I don't know where you are going, but you are getting there without any detours."[31] Nevertheless, *L'Automne à Pékin* can be easily summarized. Anne and Angel, representing the two antagonistic aspects of one and the same personality, are friends who share many things in common and are similar in a variety of ways. However, they both fall in love with Rochelle, and this event underscores the differences between them. Anne, more down-to-earth and more devoid of complexes and frustrations, becomes Rochelle's lover, while Angel must be content to love her platonically, and without any hope of possessing her. Essentially, the rivalry between the two friends becomes an unsolvable conflict which can only end in the disappearance or death of one of them. Even when Anne decides to abandon his mistress, Angel, instead of rejoicing and taking advantage of the vacuum, assassinates his friend. The story takes place in a mythical country, Exopotamie, which is mostly a desert, and to which a number of personages travel in order to build a railway system: Anne and Angel, engineers, Rochelle, a secretary, a doctor called Mangemanche, his aide, and others. Exopotamie already contains several residents, among whom are the archeologist Athanagore Porphyrogénète, his aide, Cuivre, and Pipo, owner of the hotel. The latter is killed when Ping 903, a plane built by Doctor Mangemanche, flies through the window of the hotel in its first flight test. The building itself is cut in two by the train, for it is decided that the rail lines must pass through the building, for no logical reason, since all of Exopotamie is a desert. In the ensuing collapse, all those who did not die before (Mangemanche commits suicide, Angel kills Anne and Rochelle) are buried in the débris, and the train itself disappears under the ground. There are two survivors, however, Angel and Athanagore, and the novel ends with the drawing of new plans for the building of another railway system in Exopotamie.

On the surface, there is very little that makes sense in *L'Automne à Pékin*. Why build a railway system in a country which is a desert and which is hardly inhabited? Why must the lines pass through the hotel? What are the reasons for the double killings committed by Angel at the very moment when his wishes are about to be fulfilled?

Yet, these questions, and many others that can be raised, are not devoid of answers on close examination of Vian's expertise in devising a concealed background, studded with cryptic vocabulary, as a depository of his outlook on life. Exopotamie needs a railway system precisely because it has no use for it, just as in real life buildings and cities mushroom not where needed, but where planners and developers, in their ignorance and/or selfishness, think they ought to be placed. This is in line with Vian's previously discussed experience at AFNOR, and with his abhorrence of those involved in drawings, outlines, and constructions. The building of a railway system for Exopotamie can also be viewed as a consequence of man's uncontrollable quest for the impossible, his desire for the attainment of some inexistent, luminous but essentially meaningless Graal. This is, in general, the opinion of Freddy de Vrée,[32] a view which is not necessarily excluded by Vian's constant concern with the commercial aspects of literature. What might have appealed to him was the idea of the *acte gratuit* which is implied in the pursuit of something that is at the same time difficult and needless.

A railway line must pass through the hotel perhaps because in the real world, often, neighborhoods are destroyed by bulldozers, and people are bullied out of their homes, sometimes for questionable reasons, in order to make room for superhighways or other such grandiose projects which ignore the human element in favor of the abstraction of progress.

The matter of the double killings committed by Angel is not, however, so easily explainable. In fact, the love story in *L'Automne à Pékin,* for all its subplot role in the novel, is most complex. To be sure, it is immediately obvious that Anne and Angel can be viewed as the body and soul of one and the same character: They have both attended the same school, they have had the same type of education, they have the same profession, and they both fall in love with the same woman. But while Anne is an impetuous worker, Angel loves to do nothing; whereas Anne is sensual and sure of himself, Angel is an idealist who is never satisfied; and while Anne's love for Rochelle is physical, even beastlike, that of Angel remains on a higher plane, and it can be defined best by what the French often call an *amour de tête,* that is, one which could only be diminished by intercourse.[33]

Of course, Angel is jealous of Anne, and he would like both to emulate and destroy him. His penchant for emulation is prompted by his love for Rochelle, while that for killing him is generated by his realization that he cannot continue to exist except through the elimination of the *other,* his antagonistic part, which eats away at and corrodes his spiritual being. The conflict is one of choice, and it is as old as the world: that between body and soul, between the lower and the higher aspirations of men. The assassination scene itself, as ambiguous as it is, shows nevertheless a kind of resignation on the part of Anne who practically taunts Angel into killing him, as if he were subconsciously aware of the necessary destruction of the physical by the spiritual in a world in which the former is still relegated to a position of inferiority vis-à-vis the latter:

Anne stayed close to Angel.
"How deep do you think it [the well in which Athanagore pursues his investigations] is?"
"I don't know," said Angel in a suffocated voice.
"It is deep."
Anne bent over.
"One doesn't see very much," he said. . . . "It is time."
"Not yet," said Angel, full of despair.
"Yes. Now," said Anne.
He knelt next to the opening of the well and looked deeply into the dense shadows.
"No," repeated Angel. "Not yet."
He was whispering now, and fear was obvious in his voice.
"You must get to it," said Anne. "come! Are you afraid?"
"I'm not afraid," murmured Angel.
His hand touched the back of his friend and, abruptly, he pushed him into the emptiness.

And, following the assassination, he engages in a small piece of dialogue with a friend, Amadis, to whom he makes clear the reason for, and the logic behind the murder:

"Anne is dead," he says to Amadis.
"Then, this liberates you from what," he asks?
"It frees me from myself. . . . I am awakening," Angel answers.

This awakening is, for him, a rebirth: for now the struggling duality has ended, he is no longer threatened from within, and he can view the entire antagonistic episode as a bad dream. Yet, because he can still view it as something, that is, because he still has a memory of it, it becomes also necessary to get rid of the source of the inner hostility, to kill Rochelle herself, for now she keeps teasing him: "There used to be two men who were in love with me, who fought for me; it was marvelous. It was very romanesque." Thus, the assassination of Rochelle can be viewed as the logical consequence of the murder of Anne, a consequence which makes much more sense than one which would have had him, in the absence of the rival, proceed to the conquest of the all too available object of his love.

Vian's antifeminism, to which the previous section in this chapter has alluded already, may also contain an explanation for the murder of Rochelle. Women, who in the previously discussed novel had played simply a secondary role and had been objectified matter-of-factly, are now depicted as semiuseless, temporary partners, whose need men must outgrow in a normal maturing process. In this context, the heading of Chater IX of the novel, which Vian borrowed from Baudelaire's *Fusées,* is most indicative of the author's conception of Woman's role: "To love an intelligent girl is the pleasure of a homosexual." It follows that, those who are *normal,* ought to content themselves with dull, if not idiotic exponents of the female sex. And these, because of their inferiority, must not only be discarded, but are in fact discardable. David Noakes has already observed that "Anne enjoys life as a cynic and abandons his mistress as one ejects an orange after having extracted the juice."[3][4] Cuivre herself, the female aide of Porphyrogénète, and symbol of erotic exoticism in Exopotamie for a number of inhabitants, counsels Angel not to cry on account of a girl because "girls are not worth it." And Anne, in the first chapter of the Second Part, states that one can only love a woman for a short time: a first love for two years, a second love for one year, and so on. And he goes on to explain:

"They don't have imagination. They don't have any imagination if they think they are sufficient to fill a man's life. There are so many other things. . . . This is not any less true in the case of Rochelle. There are so many other things. Even if there were nothing but this green and sharp grass. Nothing but to touch this grass or to crack between one's fingers the shell of a yellow snail, on this warm and dry sand, and to look at the small, shiny and dark grains one finds in this dry sand, and to feel it under one's fingers. . . . They don't know that there is something else.

At least very few of them know it. It's not their fault. They don't dare. They don't realize it."

And to Angel's question as to what one ought to do, or might do in the absence of the other sex, Anne, surprisingly, responds in poetic fashion. This betrays perhaps the writer's manipulation of his character; for knowing his otherwise brutish nature, one does not expect him to express himself in this manner. "To stretch on the ground," said Anne. "To be on the ground, on the sand, when it is a little windy, one's head totally empty; or to walk and to see everything, and to do things, to build stone houses for people, to give them cars, to give them light, to give them everything that people can have, so that they might be able also to do nothing and to remain on the sand, in the sun, and think of nothing, and sleep with women." This convinces Angel, for later in the novel he concludes that a conquered woman can only become a degraded woman, hence not worth having. And he tells one of his friends:

"I am not a brute. I would have dropped her before making her totally ugly. Not for me, but for her. So that she might find someone else. They have nothing except that in order to find men. Their shape. . . . When one loves a pretty woman, what one must do is to leave her, to abandon her, or to set her free before having reduced her to zero."

This is, of course, what happened in Vian's own case, for he abandoned Michelle (a number of critics saw the rhyme between Michelle and Rochelle ³⁵), for reasons already stated in the preceding chapter, a few years after his marriage.

Thus, his acute awareness of man's fragility and susceptibility to disease was further complemented by his understanding of the wearing-out process that women undergo in the arms of men. Sporadically this gave rise in him to a feeling of pity, although in his real life he did not attempt to atone for his own contribution to the *usure* of Michelle. He considered simply that such was the order of nature, that the imperfectibility of human beings precluded any possibility of change, and that love itself meant the gradual devouring of someone else. It should be recalled that physical contact, when held to a minimum, and when benefiting from the aura, albeit illusory, of an extracurricular affair, was held by the Romantics to enhance the beauty of a woman. Such was the case, for example, with Gustave Flaubert's

Emma Bovary who saw her appearance improve measurably after the
initial act of infidelity. In Vian's view, however, love, and especially
lovemaking in the course of conjugal relationships, can only result in
the boredom of the couple and in a constantly diminishing aesthetic
appreciation on the part of the man for his mate. The latter, weary of
the repetitiveness of contact, deteriorates and corrodes in her own eyes
as well, and in the eyes of others. This is the process that Rochelle
undergoes at the hands of her lover, Anne, and the results are clearly
stated by Angel:

"Whenever he touches her, her skin is no longer the same afterward.
One wouldn't say so at first, because she still looks fresh when she
comes out of Anne's arms, and her lips are just as swollen and just as
red, and her hair is just as sparkling; nevertheless she is diminished.
Each kiss that she seeks wears her out a little, and her stomach is less
firm, and her skin less smooth and less fine, and her eyes less clear, and
her walk heavier, and every day she is less and less Rochelle."

Vian's lucidity is an echo of, and is enhanced by the experiences of
his own first marriage. The lessons he learned concerning the naïve
idealism of young couples, the fact that in real life love is only taking
and cannot exist without selfishness, that there are such things as the
pain of love and the degradation of love, and the unavoidable
destruction of the female and defection of the male, are themes which,
as we shall see, are reiterated over and over again in many of his
writings. Yet, these themes, for all their assuaging sadness, are cathartic
for the reader who, constantly exposed, begins to realize that they are
not unique with him, and are not found solely within the confines of
his own rapports, but rather that they extend to all sensitive persons
whose awareness rejects illusions and delusions. Specifically, catharsis
results from the very frail, yet very feasible fraternity in similar sources
of suffering which bring together reader and writer. On a very real level,
more real than Reality, the two hold hands and console each other, and
walk together on the unsure path of the book's pages which examine
without solving and state without sentimentalizing.

Thus, the author's approach in *L'Automne à Pékin* is honest and full
of integrity. There is no deprecation of or recoil from truth, and we are
made to exit tremulously out of our own closed world of insignificant
solitude in togetherness, and to step, with care and hesitation, into that
universe discreetly poised between the tropical sky and tropical sand of
an Exopotamie which, although not on any map, draws itself, for the

reader, out of the events described in the novel. In this universe life and love are both passable and palatable in spite of the fact that there are errors of judgment (Ping 903, the futility of the railway system, its collapse and interment); that inner struggles cannot end in compromise but must resort to murder (Angel, in order to be able to uphold the spiritual qualities to which he adheres, has no solution but to become an assassin, that is to opt for the physical, to become Anne); that betrayal runs rampant (that of the engineers vis-à-vis Exopotamie, of Angel with respect to Anne, of Angel with respect to himself).

But over and above the catharsis supplied by the narration, the interest of *L'Automne à Pékin* lies also in the fact that the reader is reintroduced to familiar preoccupations of Vian, such as his anticlericalism, his scorn for medicine, and his hatred for administrators. His irreverence is obvious in the depiction of Abbé Petitjean, in whose mouth he puts the most childish pious formulae which contain high school reminiscences of Latin and, often, the silliest type of baby-play talk. In addition, Abbé Petitjean is a caricature of the devout priest. He "exercises diverse professions: layman perchance, ecclesiastic through error, militarist in order to cause laughter;" he swears constantly, and even incites his hermit, Claude Léon, to "rape Lavande, that splendid Negro girl!" It should be recalled that Petitjean stands for Grosjean, his rival and recipient of the Prix de la Pléiade which Vian had failed to get. His dislike of medicine is, of course, evident in the character of Mangemanche who is more interested in building airplanes than in practicing medicine, and whose Ping 903 flies through the hotel and kills its owner. His abhorrence of administrators can be seen in his description of the meetings of the Conseil d'Administration, meetings replete with pompous language, failing always to reach conclusions, and conducted in a turmoil that is so great that the members are completely oblivious of it. Heightening the interest of the novel are also a number of allusions to contemporaries of Vian with whom the writer had cause to disagree or quarrel. Such allusions are numerous, but suffice it to point to Ursus de Jantolent, President of the Conseil d'Administration, who in reality was a well-known personality associated with the Gallimard publishing house (and now a member of the French Academy), and to "that louse Arland," referring to Marcel Arland, editor of Gallimard at the time. It is interesting to note that for the 1956 edition of the novel Vian did not want to be so obvious in the case of Arland and respelled his name to Orland in the new manuscript he prepared. Before submitting it, however, he changed his mind, and he opined publicly that an insult which is withdrawn is the worst kind of insult.

The initial reviews of *L'Automne à Pékin* were not too enthusiastic. For example, the anonymous critic of the *Bulletin Critique du Livre Français* stated simply that the book contained "different social types which are shown under caricature traits, their adventures being funny and replete with student-like jokes: There are some plesant passages, much gracefulness in the construction of the story, but the interest is limited and there is too much facility."³ ⁶ On the contrary, when the book was reedited in 1956, this same *Bulletin Critique du Livre Français* accorded Vian a more laudatory review, stating, in part: "This original novel, which some will find bewildering, contains, in addition, a certain number of allusions which augment measurably its value."³ ⁷ At the same time, Noël Arnaud wrote: "Let the entire College pay attention to this work, let it uncover its riches: they are incalculable. A great lesson that Satrap Boris Vian gives us in *L'Automne à Pékin,* using, moreover, a sacred language."³ ⁸ And in the criticism printed at the end of the 1956 edition of the book he explained: *"L'Automne à Pékin* is one of the rare novels of our time which renders words their literal sense (a procedure pointed out already in our discussion of *Vercoquin et le plancton*) without suffering from the prejudice furnished by other possible means."³ ⁹ He went on to explain that the author's taste for semantic confusion could lead to any interpretation, as all great works ought to, and that *L'Automne à Pékin* could in effect become a classic in contemporary French literature. This is in line with the richness of the work to which he pointed in the above-mentioned article in the *Cahiers du Collège de Pataphysique.* It is interesting to note that Alain Robbe-Grillet, the future unofficial chief of the Anti-Novel school, who was working at the time as reader for the Editions de Minuit, was the one to accept Vian's manuscript. Following the advice of his reader, Jérôme Lindon, then editor of the publishing house, wrote for the cover of the novel: *"L'Automne à Pékin* could well become one of the classics of a literature which, after having exhausted with a uniformly accelerated movement all the nuances of the sinister, from Romanticism to Naturalism and from Socialism to Mysticism, notes all of a sudden that it winds up in the desert of Exopotamie; a literature where one is finally permitted to laugh!"

But, as we have seen, there is much more than laughter in *L'Automne à Pékin.* That Vian was also preoccupied with the more serious questions alluded to above is shown by the project of a short story one finds in his myriad unpublished notes in the possession of his first wife. Apparently concerned with the future of Angel after his departure from Exopotamie, he conceived making of his character the main hero of a short story that he was never to write but which he was going to call "Narcisse." The plan of this short story was outlined as follows: "He likes to receive letters. Okay. He never receives any. One day he has the idea of sending himself some. He sends himself some. The idyll becomes a fact. It grows. He makes a date with himself, under a clock, at 3 P.M. He goes to his appointment, dressed in his best clothes. And at three o'clock he commits suicide."

Thus Anne and Angel, the body and the soul, cannot coexist, but neither can Angel, the soul, go on living by himself. The inevitability of death becomes the solution of death, a pessimistic point of view recurring in different degrees of intensity in the works of Boris Vian.

IV   Les Morts ont tous la même peau

The author's third novel to appear in 1947 was published under the pseudonym of Vernon Sullivan. This was appropriate, for the narration was intended to, and in fact did treat another aspect of the problem which had been the topic of *J'irai cracher sur vos tombes.* However, *Les Morts ont tous la même peau* is not, as some critics have contended, a mere continuation of Sullivan's first published novel; nor is it, as others have imagined, a response to, or an act of vengeance against those who had attacked it. While the text is preceded by a preface in which Vian replied to the criticism leveled at *J'irai cracher sur vos tombes,* and while the hero of the new novel, Dan Parker, has the same name as the President of the Cartel d'Action Morale et Sociale who had instituted the lawsuit against author and publisher, it is noteworthy that neither is the preface unduly long or vehement in style, nor is Dan Parker depicted as an unlikable character. In fact, he is a victim, solicitous, if not deserving of our sympathy. Be it as it may, in part because of the unusual prosperity of its predecessor to which it was compared, in part because of the initial critical misunderstandings pointed to above, the book had no success at all: its various editions until 1950, when it was condemned at the same time as *J'irai cracher sur vos tombes,* are explained only by the low number of copies printed each time.

While Lee Anderson of *J'irai cracher sur vos tombes* was black and appeared white, Dan Parker is white and appears black. A bouncer in a New York nightclub, Parker is married to a white woman, Sheila, and, in general, leads the life of a white man. One day, however, a black *brother,* Richard, appears, and he threatens to tell everyone that Dan's blood is at least partially black. Enraged, the hero goes to his *brother's* house, rapes his mistress, a mulatto, as well as a Negro woman whom he meets there, in front of Richard who is drunk and whom he kills in the end. Later, followed by the police, he hides behind a curtain in his house and witnesses a dialogue between his wife and a policeman. In the course of this dialogue he learns that his father was white and that Richard had lied. The revelation purges and frees him, and it is obvious that in Vian's opinion a jury of whites would have acquitted the assassin under the circumstances. Yet, having uncovered his wife's attitude ("I would not want to remain married to a criminal," she says to the policeman before learning the truth, thereby reasserting Vian's sarcasm in the often used formula: Negro-criminal), he commits suicide.

In spite of the author's insistence on racial problems, *Les Morts ont tous la même peau* reveals only a minor interest in the rapports between whites and blacks in America. The fact is that, as in *J'irai cracher sur vos tombes,* Vian seizes on a topic which permits him to deal with themes already familiar to his readers: that of a hero concerned with his double nature;[40] that of love equated to sexuality and to possession; of adherence to impulses; of murder and suicide. In the post-World War II era, the public relishes such themes and, of course, Vian capitalizes on the vogue. The question of racism some three thousand miles away is viewed by him only as a vehicle to commercial literary success (unattained in this case), a fact which does not necessarily detract from the importance of *Les Morts ont tous la même peau* in the development of Vian as a novelist.

The narration itself lacks the impact of *J'irai cracher sur vos tombes.* Nevertheless, there are a number of passages which betray the accomplished writer by their profundity of thought expressed in simple, familiar style. When, for example, Dan Parker faces the threat of Richard's blackmail, he is so haunted, not by what he might lose materially, but by the loss of his identity which he equates with his color, that he looks in a mirror and thinks: "In front of me is a solid fellow, about thirty-five years old, big and in good health, looking at me. There is nothing to say about him. He was white without doubt...but I didn't like the expression of his eyes. ... They were the eyes of someone who had just seen a ghost." And later, while traveling in a New York subway, he looks at other passengers and compares touchingly the certainty of their destination and of their identity to the fluidity of his: "They all went someplace. They were all someone. But I was going nowhere, I was on the border between two races." In fact, the possibility of being of black origin represents such a great menace to him that sexual impotence now replaces what had been in the past an accentuated virility. The double rape of which he is guilty is only an attempt to persuade himself that his potency is what it used to be, namely, that of a complex-free white. But when lovemaking does count, such as when he returns to his wife, whom he loves, he realizes that things are not at all the same, that something has happened to his innermost fibers, that in fact he is no longer himself: "I could not do it. I couldn't do anything. Sheila didn't realize it yet, but I, I was beginning to see that I was frigid under her kisses, that her flesh did not awaken mine. . . I made desperate efforts to excite myself, to imagine erotic scenes, to dissipate that unhealthy torpor which nailed me inert on the sheets of the bed." Such passages are touching and cathartic not only because we all have some antagonistic double within us whom we fight constantly, but also because they are expressed in immediately graspable and clear terms directed to even the most mediocre sensibilities. The hero's ability to analyze his physical and spiritual reactions, in spite of the fact that he is otherwise of an impulsive and criminal nature, implies for us the very definite possibility that we, too, can equally examine ourselves and at least come close to the consolation of conclusions.

But Dan Parker's power of analysis does not stop with the mere realization of his sexual impotence. He opines correctly that, as in most similar cases, sudden lack of virility is only a symptom of more complex disorders: "My whole body was cold and flabby, my worried muscles jumped like worms under my skin which was twitching with cramps." And in his search for a solution he only manages to get himself caught in the trap of a vicious circle, for when he attempts to think of other erotic situations, or of other women, while in the arms of his wife, remorse sets in, guilt develops into a complex, and he tells himself: "I knew that I was behaving badly, and that I was doing something that I would find impossible to forgive, for I was betraying her in my spirit and my body remained insensitive to hers. . . . I went back to bed and I remained in the shadows, as if injured by something which I feared understanding only too well." What he did not wish to understand was, of course, the fact that no other solution could exist but the elimination of the double, of the *other* who was the source of the problem and whose existence precluded the possibility of his.

The only thing that Dan Parker fails to anticipate is that, once the murder of Richard is accomplished, that is, once his own identity is mended, he will find it nevertheless impossible to continue to live, for he will be unable to regain that previously experienced serenity of a man who is all one in the fullest sense of the word. Having once experienced the separations, the black from the white, the sexually impotent weakling from the highly virile male, the murderer from the law-abiding citizen, he will no longer be capable of accepting the state of repair which his identity will undergo at the expense of Richard's death. The fact that Sheila was ready to give up on him, that she in fact began to flirt with the policeman, are only the immediate explanations which he needs to have in order to give some plausibility to his reasons for suicide. The attentive reader, however, understands that there are other, more basic causes, which make it impossible for Dan Parker to survive: a man's makeup cannot be the result of a mending job, and what was whole and sound cannot regain its unity and wholesomeness by means of illegal expedients which promote only artificially a state of recovery. And so, "Dan appeared to come out from a dream. With a slow, inexorable gesture, he climbed on the window's ledge and bent in order to be able to jump. He noticed below, far away on the road, a compact group of people and, instinctively, he maneuvered his body in order to avoid them. He turned in the air like a clumsy frog and crashed on the hard surface of the street."

Largely ignored or dismissed by the critics, *Les Morts ont tous la même peau* reveals, nevertheless, the author's ability to reweave popular plots while at the same time managing to appeal also to those members of the literary elite who are willing to read between the lines, as it were, to uncover the author's brilliant preoccupations which hide under the appearances of a mere best seller. David Noakes admired the simplicity of the novel,[41] and Michel Rybalka noted the possible influence of Albert Camus' *L'Etranger,* a story in which the hero also dies because of a misunderstanding.[42] The critic does not elaborate, nor does he give any specific instances of similarity; however, it is known that Vian was a friend of Camus, and that Camus visited the Vians many times in their home.

Few others have had anything to say about *Les Morts ont tous la même peau,* but in view of its scandal-causing predecessor, *J'irai cracher sur vos tombes,* the fact is not surprising.

V L'Ecume des jours

Although fragments of the novel had appeared a year earlier in *Les Temps modernes,* Gallimard's original edition was published in 1947, a year which, as we know, saw the appearance of several other works signed either Boris Vian or Vernon Sullivan. The typed manuscript of the story, now in the possession of his first wife, is signed with the pseudonym Bison Duravi, and the book is dated "Memphis, 8 March 1946; Davenport, 10 March 1946," places which, of course, Vian had never visited. As mentioned in the previous chapter, the book was dedicated to Michelle: *Pour mon Bibi,* he had written, but in a more extensive, inked dedication to his wife, he had added that *L'Ecume des jours* had been composed because of the "impatience which I feel for being judged on something else besides the childishness of *Vercoquin.*" It will be recalled that, when the manuscript of the novel was submitted to Gallimard in 1946, the author was considered for it as a possible recipient of the Prix de la Pléiade which, eventually, was given to Jean Grosjean. The publication was one of the more successful works of Boris Vian. Various other printings were published after the author's death: two in 1963 alone, one in 1965, another in 1967. The novel was translated under the title of *Chloe* in Germany, *Froth on the Daydream* in England, and as *Mood Indigo* in the United States. A play adaptation was successfully presented in Brussels in 1968, and in the course of the same year it was transposed to the screen.

The brief Foreword which precedes the text merits inclusion here for it provides a clue to the various meanings of the novel and to Vian's philosophy of life especially insofar as Existentialism and *engagement* are concerned:

The essential thing in life is to judge everything *a priori.* It would seem, in fact, that the masses are wrong and individuals always right. But we must be careful not to deduce from that any rules about how to behave; these should not need to be formulated for us to follow them. There are only two things: love, all sorts of love, with pretty girls, and the music of New Orleans or Duke Ellington. Everything else ought to go, because everything else is ugly, and the few pages of proof which follow derive all their strength from the fact that this is a completely true story, since I imagined it from start to finish. Properly speaking its material realization consists in projecting reality obliquely and enthusiastically onto another surface which is irregularly corrugated and so distorts everything. As you can see, if ever there was a procedure that does us credit, this is it.[43]

Before going into the story of *L'Ecume des jours,* and in order to understand the quotation above, especially those sentences which reveal the author's abhorrence of the masses and of those who cater to them instead of pursuing the cult of the individual, it is necessary first to elaborate on Vian's relationship with the Sartre-Simone de Beauvoir couple.[44]

While only rarely philosophically close to the ideas of Sartre and de Beauvoir, the Vians had both professional and social ties with them. The articles which Vian wrote for *Les Temps modernes* kept him in constant touch with the ascending fame of Sartre, fame which in the late 1940's began to spread throughout the world, but especially within the Parisian literary and philosophical circles. In fact, when Vian began to write *L'Ecume des jours,* Sartre's reputation was such that he became a living legend, a sort of demigod that people looked up to, listened to avidly, and emulated almost without question. According to Vian's mother, Boris thought for many years that *La Nausée* was one of the greatest novels ever written in French, and it was perhaps this mixture of genuine admiration and distaste for the gross love that masses are capable of which made him introduce into the novel, parallel to a love story to be mentioned later, what he called the Partrian theme: for this theme, instead of Jean-Paul Sartre, he names one of the more important characters Jean-Sol Partre, while Simone de Beauvoir becomes, in *L'Ecume des jours,* the Duchess of Bovouart. The Partrian story (about which more later) was both an homage and a *dig* to the two celebrated apostles of Existentialism.

Of course, Sartre could not have possibly appreciated Vian's public declaration: "I am not an Existentialist. In fact, for an Existentialist, existence precedes essence. For me, there is no essence."[4 5] Nevertheless, both he and Simone de Beauvoir read the manuscript of *L'Ecume des jours,* and liked it. Sartre, who was a member of the jury for the Prix de la Pléiade, gave Vian his support in what turned out to be, subsequently, a losing cause. His appreciation of Vian as a writer was seconded by that of his friend, for she wrote in *La Force des choses:* "I met Vian at the bar of Pont-Royal; he had given to Gallimard a manuscript [that of the novel] which I and Queneau liked very much."[4 6]

In addition, as alluded to above, the professional relationship between the Vians and the Sartre-de Beauvoir couple was supplemented by strong social ties. Sartre and Simone attended many parties in the home of the Vians, and in fact one of the best portraits left to us of the writer is that which Simone wrote in *La Force des choses:*

When I arrived, everyone had already drunk too much; his wife, Michelle, her long white silk hair falling on her shoulders, was smiling to the angels; Astruc [a fellow Zazou] was sleeping on the sofa, shoeless; I also drank valiantly while listening to records imported from America. Around two in the morning Boris offered me a cup of coffee; we sat in the kitchen and until dawn we talked: about his novel, on jazz, on literature, about his profession as engineer. I found no affectation in his long, white and smooth face, only an extreme gentleness and a kind of stubborn candor; Vian detested just as passionately *les affreux* [the masses] as he adored those whom he loved; he played the trumpet, although his heart was giving him trouble ("If you continue, you will be dead in ten years," the doctor had told him). We spoke, and dawn arrived only too quickly. I had the highest appreciation, when I had the chance of enjoying them, for these fleeting moments of eternal friendship.[47]

On the other hand, Sartre's personal relationship with the Vians was not always pleasant. It appears that he was more attracted by the personality of Michelle than by that of her husband. While Vian was never jealous, he wondered often why, when his marriage began to break up, Sartre would always take the part of Michelle. In fairness to Sartre, it should be pointed out that, when he was asked to umpire a conflict between the two spouses, he had to take someone's side, and in view of Boris' obvious eccentricities and Michelle's equally obvious sedateness, it was more plausible for him to defend the latter. Sartre's later liaison with Michelle did not come about until after Vian had left his wife and had moved in with Ursula Kübler. Simone de Beauvoir is precise on the timing of Sartre's relationship with his friend's wife: "Michelle had separated from Boris, and Sartre, who had always found her very attractive, began then to see her regularly."[48] In spite of this liaison, however, and owing either to Vian's gentleness noted by Simone de Beauvoir, or to the fact that he himself desired a definitive break from Michelle, his rapports with Sartre did not worsen appreciably. Noël Arnaud, who made a rather complete investigation of the circumstances in question, wrote: "Boris saw Sartre twice during those years [in the early 1950's]. Embarrassment or sarcasm, in the course of these meetings which are clothed in the appearance of the greatest cordiality...Sartre will conclude that Boris does not particularly seek his company."[49] Thus, there was no quarrel or open break, and the two managed to hold on to a relationship which, although cold, continued for a number of years. To Sartre's thoughts, considered dialectic and totalitarian, Vian simply opposed his love for the imagination of man and the rights of the individual. If such an attitude left him open to the risk of a reproach of superficiality, he accepted it and, in the "Partrian" theme of *L'Ecume des jours,* he showed brilliantly that the opposite direction, that of Existentialism, is just as vulnerable.

To prove his point, Vian invented the character of Chick, a personage who is fanatically Existentialist. He looks up to Partre, bestows upon him divine-like qualities, and buys and collects everything that he writes. Some of Partre's titles which he relishes are: *Le Paradoxe sur le Dégueulis, Le Choix préalable avant le haut-le-coeur, Le Vomi, Le Remugle, Renvoi de fleurs,* and others, works which are all parodies of Sartre's celebrated theme of nausea. To others, who try to persuade Chick that he ought not to spend all his money for Partre's books, he replies: "How can one not be interested in a man such as Partre? Capable of writing on any subject, of writing anything, and with what precision!" His love for Partre's books is not simply limited to the material they contain, but extends also to their physical format. For example, he binds one of the volumes "in leather of nothingness," which is in line with one of Vian's projects in 1946 when he circulated among his and Sartre's friends a petition which requested funds for a statue of Sartre which would have represented him as "a nice adolescent seated on a huge block of nothingness." Moreover, he collects Partre's old pipes and all his pyjamas. In his fanaticism he forgets about the woman he loves, Alise, whom he cannot marry for lack of money, and to whom all he can give is a ring "in the shape of nausea." This, despite the fact that one of his friends, Colin, lends him twenty-five thousand francs in order that he be able to marry Alise (money which he uses entirely to appease his appetite for Partre's works). Alise, at one point, aware of the fact that Partre is going to publish a very voluminous and expensive series entitled *L'Encyclopédie de la nausée,* decides to appeal to the author to slow down, so that her fiancé will have a chance to postpone his total financial ruin. Thereupon an intriguing and engaging piece of dialogue takes place:

Over Jean-Sol's shoulder she could see the heading, *Encyclopedia,* Volume Nineteen. She placed a timid hand on Jean-Sol's arm; he stopped writing.
"You've got that far already," said Alise.
"Yes," replied Jean-Sol. "Did you want to speak to me?"
"I want to ask you not to publish it," she said.
"That's difficult," said Jean-Sol. "People are waiting for it."
He took off his glasses, breathed on the lenses and put them on again; his eyes were no longer visible.
"Of course," said Alise. "But I only meant you will have to delay it."
"Oh," said Jean-Sol, "if that's all, we might be able to do something."
"You will have to delay it for ten years," said Alise.
"Really?" said Jean-Sol.

"Yes," said Alise. "Ten years, or longer of course. It would be better to let people save up, you know, so that they will be able to buy it."

"It'll be pretty tedious to read," said Jean-Sol Partre, "because I've already found it very tedious writing it. I've got severe cramp in the left wrist from holding the paper."

"I'm sorry for your sake," said Alise.

"That I have cramps?"

"No," said Alise. "That you won't hold up publication."

"Why?"

"I will explain: Chick spends all his money buying what you write and he hasn't got any more money."

"He would do better to buy something else," said Jean-Sol. "I never buy my own books."

"He likes what you write."

"He has a right to," said Jean-Sol. "He's made his choice."

It is clear then, that there are also dangers in closed philosophical systems and in their enunciation which spreads and grips naïve followers who fail to discern the good from the bad, and who equate the beauty or the veracity of a philosopher's tenets with the cover of his books or with his petty personal possessions. And so, Alise, convinced that Partre is right in that Chick has "made his choice" and is therefore totally *engagé* elsewhere, has no recourse but to kill the philosopher whom she holds responsible for her misfortunes. She "summoned up her strength and with a determined gesture planted the heart-extractor in Partre's chest. He looked at her; he died very quickly, and gave a last look of astonishment when he discovered his heart was tetrahedral in shape. Alise turned very pale, Jean-Sol Partre was now dead and the tea was getting cold. She took the manuscript of the *Encyclopedia* and tore it up."

An even more burlesque type of description of the Existentialist movement as a whole, and of Sartre in particular, is given by the author in the passage which describes the philosopher's now famous conference on Existentialism which he gave in October, 1945, at the Club Maintenant. Simone de Beauvoir herself, in *La Force des choses,* noted that, "at Sartre's conference, there came such a crowd that the space would not hold it: there was a frightful skirmish and some women fainted."[50] Vian's burlesque tone in his accounting of the meeting notwithstanding, his description is not too far removed from the truth:

Some arrived by hearse and the policemen plunged a long steel pike into the coffins, nailing them to the oak for ever and ever, which meant that they did no one any harm except the people who would one day die properly and whose shrouds had been ruined. Others got themselves parachuted in from special planes (they were fighting at Le Bourget too, to get on the planes). A squad of firemen used these as targets, and diverted them with their hoses toward the Seine, where they drowned miserably. Others, finally, tried to get there through the sewers. They were driven back by being kicked on the knuckles with hobnailed boots, just as they gripped the edge of the manholes in order to get their strength back and climb out, and the rats took care of the rest. But nothing could discourage such zealots. It must, however, be admitted that those who were drowned and those who persevered in their attempts were not the same ones. The noise mounted to the heavens, reverberating from the clouds with a hollow rumbling.

Later, Jean-Sol Partre is described as entering on an elephant's back, much like a fakir, and he begins his speech among "countless cases of fainting, due to the intrauterine exultation which overcame the female members of the audience particularly." Partre's speech cannot be heard by anyone because of the enthusiasm of the crowd and the noise of photographers and newsreel reporters. Nevertheless, he does manage to show to the audience "samples of stuffed vomit," another obvious pun on Sartre's famous *La Nausée*. At the end, the entire roof of the structure collapses into the hall, and "among the plaster, whitish shapes stirred, staggered about, and then collapsed, asphyxiated by the heavy cloud which floated above the debris." At this point, Partre, delighted, begins to slap his thighs and to laugh heartily, "happy to see so many 'engaged' people."

Vian's tone, then, is such that perhaps only minimal and informal criticism of Existentialism and its followers can be deduced from the above. In fact, others delighted at the time in equally parodical descriptions of the goings-on in which the Rive Gauche became involved.[51] What is clear, however, is that the author's statements in the Foreword of *L'Ecume des jours* must be taken with a grain of salt, for at least some of the events in the novel are not entirely of his invention. His projection of reality "obliquely and enthusiastically onto another surface which is irregularly corrugated and so distorts everything," would also seem to indicate, given the deliberateness of the procedure, that Vian did not harbor any strong or systematic animosity toward Sartre. As a matter of fact, Simone de Beauvoir did not see any maliciousness on the part of the author, for the 14 May entry in *La Force des choses* contains only a compliment: "His novel is extremely amusing, especially the conference of Jean-Sol Partre and the murder with the heart-extractor."[52] To have opposed the great master or his movement any more than he did in his novel, would have constituted in itself a type of *engagement* and, of course, his temperament was totally unsuited for it.

In fact, *L'Ecume des jours* is primarily a love story. Freddy de Vrée, for example, ignores almost entirely the fun that Vian has at the expense of Existentialism, and concentrates on the love plot. He summarizes the novel as follows: "Colin loves Chloé who becomes sick and dies. Colin commits suicide and his rat commits suicide also. As plot, it is, happily, rather thin."[53] The jacket of the novel itself ignores also the subplot described above and advertises only the love story: "Colin meets Chloé. They fall in love. They get married. Chloé becomes sick. Colin bankrupts himself to cure her. The doctor cannot cure her. Chloé dies. Colin will not live much longer afterwards." But there is much more. The couple Colin-Chloé goes through all the exciting and terrible stages of a passionate love which, when it is as strong as in their case, must, of necessity, end in death. The fact that the author of *Vercoquin et le plancton* and of *L'Automne à Pékin* gives us now a touching and pathetic description of marital love is indeed surprising, for it reveals a Vian heretofore unknown, and consequently all the more intriguing. That is not to say that the love story of Colin and Chloé is not replete with typical Vianesque situations. For example, Chloé's disease is caused by a nenuphar which grows in her lungs. As her malady progresses, and she gets closer and closer to death, the apartment in which the couple lives becomes smaller and smaller. When she dies, the apartment collapses, and roof and floor join miraculously. One recognizes, of course, in all of this, the author's acute awareness of the diminishing process which life undergoes in the face of disease, ending in total annihilation in the face of death.

There are other events which might tend to make the unobserving and careless reader laugh, but for which Vian had different intentions. When Chick, for instance, attempts to put a tie on Colin's neck, and the knot grips his finger and crushes it, it is obvious that the writer meant to point to man's dependence on things lifeless which, participating in life as they do, hamper and diminish the existence of the animate. Other miraculous events, too, are less intended to cause laughter than to indicate the hostility and the brutal force of objects. When Colin puts on one of Ellington's records entitled *The Mood to Be Wooed,* the o's on the label cause the corners of the room to become round. Later on, the door to the apartment becomes so narrow that it is difficult to pass through it. As Chloé weakens more and more, the bed on which she lies gets closer and closer to the ground. In the shop where Chick works, the workers are attached by steel chains to their machines which constantly attack them (in fact, four of the workers have their hands cut at the wrist by the machines). Chloé's funeral is a particularly nightmarish event replete with a violence that the participants are unable to prevent: the coffin is thrown out of a window and breaks the leg of a child playing nearby, while one of the pallbearers barely escapes being strangled by the strap around the coffin and attached to his neck. Vian's poetic vision makes it possible even for a flower to become the direct cause of a human's death, and these are all events which anticipate by many years similarly strange happenings in the Anti-Novel and Anti-Theatre of the 1950's and 1960's.

The only difference appears to be that, while such writers as Samuel Beckett and Eugène Ionesco delve in a purely cadaveric[54] universe, the world of Boris Vian retains a slapstick quality which is cathartic, if not less pessimistic. In addition, as he specifies in his Foreword, some things in life do remain worthwhile: love and jazz, for example. There are many passages in *L'Ecume des jours* which could serve to show this slightly more hopeful, more lyrical approach to life, but suffice it to point to an especially poetic one in which Vian describes how the rats in Colin's apartment like to dance to the sound of the sun's rays on the kitchen faucets, and how they run after the tips of the rays which come gaily through the windows and end up pulverized on the floor. Such merriment sustains Chloé, at least temporarily, and it is only when her malady becomes acute that the dancing ceases and the sun's rays simply stretch on the ground in thin and lazy flaccidness. It is fitting, then, given the previous friendship between them, that the only rat to remain alive at the time of Chloé's death, after escaping from the collapsing building, set "off in the direction of the cemetery." There, in a moving scene which symbolizes man's ultimate acquiescence and capitulation, he offers himself to the seemingly indifferent, yet always frightening cat:

"It really doesn't appeal to me very much," said the cat.
"You're making a mistake," said the mouse. "I'm still young and I was well fed right up to the last minute."
"But I'm well fed too," said the cat, "and I haven't the least desire to commit suicide, so you can see why I find it abnormal."

But in the dialogue which continues, the mouse manages to convince the cat that suicide is the only solution (or lack thereof) which remains available. Whereupon the cat, standing for a rapacious, devouring universe, *gives in:*

"Well," said the cat, "if that's the case, I'm quite ready to render you my services, but I don't know why I'm saying 'if that's the case' because I don't even begin to understand."
"You're very kind," said the mouse.
"Put your head in my mouth," said the cat, "and wait."
"Will it take a long time?" asked the mouse.
"Until someone steps on my tail," said the cat. "I need a quick reflex action. But I'll leave it sticking out, don't worry."
The mouse parted the cat's jaws and stuck his head between the sharp teeth. . . . He closed his little black eyes. . .the cat carefully allowed his sharp canines to rest on the soft, grey neck. The mouse's black whiskers mingled with his own. He unfurled his bushy tail and spread it across the pavement.

Thus, the relationship between living creatures, human or nonhuman, is beautifully evoked by the author in his description of the friendly rat's suicide. The fact that the last line of the novel states: "Toward them, singing, came eleven little blind girls from the Orphanage of Julius the Apostolic," pointing to the indifference of the universe as expressed by exponents of the Church, demonstrates Vian's ability to provide the necessary comic relief one is ready for at the end of the story.

But beyond this ability, in the aforementioned line, as well as in numerous other passages, Vian pursues his virulent, if comic attacks against religion which he feels is an unworthy palliative sold expensively to unsuspecting men. For example, he makes a point to say that since religious interments cost too much, Colin is obliged to bury Chloé in a cemetery for the poor, while passersby carelessly sing a tune entitled *A la salade,* whose words are most questionable for the occasion. And Jesus himself, who attends the burial, does nothing but yawn. In fact, he has been made sleepy by a dialogue in which he had engaged with Colin right after Chloé's death:

He [Colin] raised his eyes: in front of him, fixed to the wall, was Jesus on his cross. He looked bored and Colin asked him:
"Why did Chloe die?"
"It's got nothing to do with me," said Jesus. "Suppose we talk about something else."
"Whose responsibility is it?" asked Colin.
They were conversing in very low tones and the others could not hear what they were saying.

"Not ours, in any case," said Jesus.

"I invited you to our wedding," said Colin.

"It was good," said Jesus, "I enjoyed it. Why didn't you spend more money this time [for the burial]?"

"I haven't got any left," said Colin, "and anyway, I'm not getting married this time."

"I see," said Jesus.

He seemed embarrassed. . . .

"Why did you make her die?" asked Colin.

"Oh!" said Jesus. "Don't keep this up."

He tried to make himself more comfortable on his nails.

"She was so sweet," said Colin, "She never did anything wrong in either thought or deed."

"That's got nothing to do with religion."

And to Colin's mild but final words of revolt, "I can't see what we've done. . .we didn't deserve this," Jesus, like the Servant at the end of Camus' play *The Misunderstanding,* maintains an impassable silence: "Jesus did not reply. Colin looked up again. Jesus' chest rose and fell gently and regularly. His features breathed calm. His eyes had closed and Colin could hear, coming from his nostrils, a faint purr of satisfaction, like a well-fed cat." The metaphysical problem of the confrontation between a God who, in His extreme goodness, ought to abolish the suffering of the innocent, and the disease and death of a guiltless human being, has always been central to Christianity, whether under the pen of an adversary of it, such as Voltaire in his poem *Le Désastre de Lisbonne,* or in most any other of his writings, or under that of a defender of Christianity like Dostoevski in *The Brothers Karamazov.* Vian, while clothing the problem in comical tones, that is, while handling it lightly, is not any less serious in his basic awareness of it: throughout his life, on paper, in speeches, and in conversations recalled by friends and relatives, he had consistently viewed religion as an insult to the intelligence of man who, in his lucidity, ought to reject any facile solutions for anything that is absurd, or unjust, or incomprehensible still.

While Vian's animosity for religion may have cost him some readers in the years immediately following the War, when there was a national, indeed an international revival of religious feelings, *L'Ecume des jours* was nevertheless an immediate success. Not only did it cause the jury of the Prix de la Pléiade to consider him as a possible recipient, but also the initial reviews were almost unanimously laudatory. Jean Blanzat, for example, wrote: "Everything is transposed, each episode, each detail is treated under an allegorical form by comparison to which the language of Giraudoux appears to be nearly Balzacian. . . . It is a miracle that, in spite of so many strange things, of researched oddities, of verbal acrobatics, one still hears a true voice, and that, after some effort, one can follow the narrative of Chloé and Colin as one does a moving, if banal love story."[55] The usually conservative Emile Henriot stated: "Certain pages of *L'Ecume des jours,* and many playful others, have touched me. Watch out for humorists. They don't always succeed in annihilating in them the elegist."[56] Henriot's appreciation is particularly correct if one keeps in mind the physical diminishment and/or destruction of surroundings in *L'Ecume des jours,* as well as the violent death of many of its protagonists: Alise assassinates, Partre at first, then a number of bookstore owners; she herself is killed in a fire; the nenuphar eats away at Chloé's body until there is little left to inter; Colin commits suicide. Later critics too were unanimous in praising "this admirable book which *L'Ecume des jours* is."[57] David Noakes, for example, while cautioning that the characters might deceive the reader who seeks in the novel *real* personages of the type with whom he is familiar, admires nevertheless Vian's work and labels it as "a book one cannot forget."[58] Jacques Bens, in a post scriptum to the J.-J. Pauvert edition of the novel, corroborates Henriot's earlier opinion that *L'Ecume des jours* is very close to tragedy, and points out that its format is classical in conception. He dwells on the rigorously logical unfolding of the two plots, that of the Partrian theme and that of the love story between Colin and Chloé. Indeed, in "this the most poignant contemporary love novel"[59] there is a profound unity which brings very close together the two couples, Chick-Alise, threatened by Partre, an intellectual cancer, and Colin-Chloé, endangered by a physical one. In both cases the menace is dual, that is, exterior and interior, as it is in the best examples of ancient tragedy: Partre and the nenuphar are dangers from the outside insinuating themselves into the life of the characters, the first in the mind of Chick, the second in the lung of Chloé. And from their blind and deadly onslaught there is no retreat, as indeed in real life there is no escape either from mental anguish or from one's physical suffering. The two, singly or together, must bring about the total destruction of the individual, and this is one facet of the novel which critics often praised, for it reveals admirably the serious, pathetic side of an author sometimes thought of as merely one other Pataphysician.

It will be recalled that in his preface the writer cautions readers not to draw any moral out of his story. Yet, in an unpublished note on

L'Ecume des jours, Vian's words are so clear that it is almost impossible
not to deduce a subtle suggestion towards at least one major attitude
worth having in life: "In the preface, don't forget to recall that there
are two periods, that in which one dresses carefully, when life consists
in getting dressed almost all the time, that is before one gets married,
and one watches, on Saturday night, the appearance of the pimple that
one will have on one's nose on Sunday, and then another period when
one is more tranquil, that is to say when one begins to be unhappy
because one has stopped thinking of oneself only."[60] There is a lesson
of rugged individualism to be learned from the above: namely, that, if
Chick had not been a Partrian, and Colin did not fall in love with Chloé,
things might have turned out differently or, at least, a calamitous
outcome in the case of each would have been postponed. But the
impact of this lesson must be tempered and modified by the evidence
that one cannot always worry about one's pimples on one's nose; for
even if there are only two things that are worthwhile, love and music,
they too must be sought and pursued outside of one's own company.
And so, the dangers of sociability notwithstanding, one must step out
of one's own vacuum, if tremulously and with the greatest care, in
order to reach those very few and very elusive values which give
meaning, temporarily, to one's existence. Thus, Vian's persistently
gloomy outlook on life, stabilized by and petrified in his own infirmity
and impending death, is not any different in *L'Ecume des jours* from
that perceived in the previous novels, as indeed it will not differ
appreciably from that of his subsequent fiction.

VI   Et on tuera tous les affreux

Vian's third title to be published under the pseudonym of Vernon
Sullivan appeared first in installments in *France-Dimanche.* In spite of
the publicity given to it, it soon became evident that, in view of its
scandalous nature and the letters of protest received by the newspaper,
a commercial success was out of the question. In fact, *France-Dimanche*
dropped the publication of the novel which was later accepted by the
Editions du Scorpion with the caption "translated from American by
Boris Vian." In its 1960 printing, however, authorship was attributed to
Boris Vian, and there was no mention of Vernon Sullivan. On the
contrary, for the 1964, 1965 and 1967 editions the author of the novel
became once more Vernon Sullivan.

The initial interest of the book was probably prompted by the fact
that almost all the characters are modeled upon friends or

acquaintances of Vian: for example, Mike Bokanski stands for Michel Bokanowski; Jef Devay for J. F. Devay, a reporter for *Combat;* Ozéus Pottar was in fact the pseudonym of Jean Suyeux; Douglas Thruk, who in the novel works on an *esthetic of Cinema,* is none other than the famous cineast Alexandre Astruc; and Dr. Markus Schutz was the diminutive of Marco Schutzenberger, director of research services at Companie Nationale de Recherches Scientifiques. Because it was initially destined for a newspaper, Vian's tone, in spite of the protesters, remained mild by comparison to the previous titles which had appeared under the pseudonym of Vernon Sullivan. But once the newspaper stopped the publication of the work, Vian rewrote it with the usual brio that readers of Vernon Sullivan had come to expect. As we shall see, the story lent itself to the treatment of themes dear to and previously successful for the writer: police pursuits, science fiction, pornography, and, as always with Vian, an underlying philosophical question not always clearly stated but sempiternally present and transcending the surface descriptions and dialogues.

The action takes place in California where Rock Bailey, the narrator, has just been elected "Mr. Los Angeles." He exemplifies muscular, masculine beauty, a quality which he has decided to preserve by remaining a virgin until age twenty. The fact that he is handsome, coupled with his determination to resist the verbal and not so verbal assaults of young and not so young admirers, places him in a series of pornographically erotic situations until he falls prey to the appetites of the nymphomaniac Sunday Love. His various adventures lead him to the property of a certain Dr. Markus Schutz, whose work consists in attempting to better the human race by means of "selecting beautiful boys and beautiful girls and causing them to reproduce." His efforts result in a number of robots of exceptional beauty and intelligence, the best of whom is Jef Devay, Vian's friend at the *Combat.* Jef Devay is so above the other robots that he could not condescend to communicate or copulate with any of them, so he has no choice but to masturbate continuously. Dr. Schutz's explanation for his life's work is:

People are all very ugly. Have you noticed that one cannot walk in the streets without seeing lots of ugly people? Well, I love to walk in the streets, but I abhor ugliness. So I have built a street of my own and I have manufactured pretty passersby. . . . It was the simplest thing to do. I have earned much money by curing billionaires full of stomach ulcers. . . . But I have enough. . . . Up to my neck. . . . Insofar as I am concerned there is only one slogan: all the frightful [ugly] ones shall be killed. . . .It's kind of funny, isn't it?

Schutz's theories, Hitlerian in nature, are soon recognized as such, and his hunger for power is obvious in the fact that he wishes to become President of the United States and has begun already to place his own men in the government. But Rock Bailey and his friends at the F.B.I. pursue Dr. Schutz on a small Pacific island where a battle is about to take place between them and the handsome male and female robots who inhabit it. A showdown is averted, however, when an experiment points unexpectedly to the futility of a philosophy of Aestheticism replacing one based on traditional moral values. For this experiment, twenty-five of the most beautiful males of the American Marine are selected, and twenty-five others "so ugly and so paltry that they could cause the milk of a Texas cow to turn." Before these fifty men are placed fifty of Dr. Schutz's female specimens. And, to the surprise of all, forty-seven of the fifty assault the group of ugly men, while only three get hold of the others, more specifically, one marine "built like Hercules and covered with black hairs like a Satyr." The conclusion suggested is that, too beautiful themselves and too saturated by handsome men, the women choose those who are different and therefore unknown. Schutz, the prophet of a new world, is unmasked as a false prophet, and Aestheticism is shown to be incapable of solving any basic human problems.

When he was able to daydream, Vian told how he would have liked to be the type of prophet Schutz was unable to incarnate,

> He who thinks only in verses
> And writes only in music
> On diverse subjects
> Red and green ones
> But always magnificent.[6] [1]

He realized, of course, that this was an impossible dream, just as that of Dr. Schutz was. Condemned to live in a physical world, man is naturally tempted by Aestheticism which becomes for him a consolation for a world limited to sensations, and at the same time an ideal, magnifying and purifying the objects of one's senses. In the same collection quoted above, the poet evoked touchingly the question and the answer implied in the effort or justification of the physical by giving to it an aura of spirituality:

> Why do I live?
> Why do I live?
> For the yellow thigh
> Of a blonde woman

> Leaning on a wall
> Under a blazing sun.
>
> . . . .
>
> Why do I live?
> Because it is pretty.[62]

Et on tuera tous les affreux contains, then, a number of Vianesque themes previously encountered in the other novels signed with the pseudonym Vernon Sullivan. It lacks, however, the social considerations which he had included, or some thought he had included, in the preceding two titles. Perhaps because of this, outside of the initial scandal caused by the identification of characters with living personages, the book had passed almost unnoticed. "The third endeavor of Vernon Sullivan is not the least ingenious,"[63] was one of the typically mild and hardly laudatory critical comments at the time of the novel's publication. Likewise, later reviewers of Vian's works have had little to say about *Et on tuera tous les affreux.* David Noakes alone admired the author's treatment of the libidinous theme for its lack of any transcendental pretensions, such as found in Henry Miller and Jean Genet. In fact, Vian always appears to make of eroticism a mere concession to the middle class, and to the middle-class characteristics harbored even by the literary elite. For example, the orgy in which the experiment mentioned above results is described with such burlesque tones that the sexual details cannot help but amuse, and only amuse.

VII   Elles se rendent pas compte

Libidinousness is also used for amusing purposes in the last novel to be published under the pen name of Vernon Sullivan. In fact, *Elles se rendent pas compte* appeared without any mention of Boris Vian who either did not want to take any more chances after his condemnation for the authorship of *J'irai cracher sur vos tombes* or, in view of the general weakness of the narrative, found it impractical to let it be known that he was indeed its creator.

Vian's bibliographers have disagreed in the past on the publication date of the book: some have indicated the year 1948 which is, for yet unexplained reasons, the copyright date of the novel; others have been able to prove that *Elles se rendent pas compte* was written in 1948 but published only two years later by the Editions du Scorpion. Vian himself pointed out that in the course of 1948 he was at work on two titles, one good, the other bad, the former being *L'Herbe rouge,* the latter *Elles se rendent pas compte.*[64] The writer's appreciation of the quality of Sullivan's last title proved to be correct, for indeed in 1950 it received no reviews and it seems that it went almost entirely unnoticed until it was reedited by *Le Terrain Vague* in 1965, with Boris Vian indicated at that time as the translator of Vernon Sullivan.

The narration contains the usual Vianesque dosage of alcohol, sexuality, drugs, and murders. The central character is Francis Deacon, somewhat of a forerunner of Goldfinger, a former Harvard student who, together with his friend, Ritchie, attempts to save the life of Gaya Valenko, a young girl who is about to be victimized by a band of lesbians headed by Louise Walcott. To facilitate the penetration of the lesbian group, Francis and Ritchie put on feminine clothes, and thus the theme of travesty reappears in *Elles se rendent pas compte.* It will be recalled that in *J'irai cracher sur vos tombes* Lee Anderson was a black who passed for white; in *Les morts ont tous la même peau,* Dan Parker was a white who believed he was black; and in *Et on tuera tous les affreux,* numberless robots passed for humans.[65] But while disguising oneself may be initially a necessary submission to a practical imperative, it is later clear that one may easily become complacent about or even enamored of the new pose. "I have fallen in love with myself," tells the hero after admiring himself in the mirror just prior to going to a costume ball where a girl, dressed as a boy, picks him up. The result of this encounter is, of course, the one expected, and it conforms adequately to complications and solutions usually associated with sexual situations treated with burlesque overtones. Vian himself had said once:

> I should not want to die. . .
> Without having tried to wear a dress
> On the Grands Boulevards[66]

which indicated, perhaps, a serious desire on the part of the poet to live out a burlesque situation, no matter how ludicrous (as in fact he did on numerous occasions in his parallel existence as the *Prince de Saint-Germain-des-Prés).*

The fortunes of the two friends within the lesbian camp are replete with erotic encounters which place them in a favorable, if not enviable position. "They are quite content with us," says the narrator in Chapter XI. "From a moral point of view, of course, because, for these poor girls it is a good deed to give back to them a taste for normal lovemaking. . . . It's true, they don't realize it." The other complications of the intrigue, murders, suicides, and so on, manage to provide for a certain amount of suspense in spite of their lack of plausibility. It is only the author's art, that is, the swiftness of the narrative process, which makes one ignore the absence of verisimilitude, a procedure which Vian had mastered in the course of his work as real translator of a number of American detective writers such as Kenneth Fering, Raymond Chandler, Peter Cheyney, and James Cain. Lack of literary validity notwithstanding, the novel is nevertheless palatable, for in addition to the procedure mentioned above, it also contains a number of contemporary allusions replete with comico-serious remarks. For example, in Chapter XI, Francis Deacon explains in the following manner why he cannot go into certain details of a love scene: "There are some very representative aspects which are particularly pleasant but for which it is forbidden to make any propaganda, because one has the right to excite people to killing, in Indochina or elsewhere, but not to encourage them to make love." Of course, the fact that there is little logic in these statements does not detract from the pleasure of the reader of fiction for whom such thorny real problems as one's attitude toward censorship or one's views regarding war are of special contemporary relevance.

Elles se rendent pas compte contains also, more than any other novel, a strong expression of Vian's misogyny. It will be recalled that the deterioration of his own marriage had begun prior to the conception of this novel, and that in previous compositions he had already relegated women to positions of inferiority or had objectified them in various degrees. In the present narrative they are depicted not only as abnormal and criminal, but they are simply shown to be bloodthirsty cannibals. While the tone remains in a lampoon, and while there is always a suspicion that one is only faced with a tongue-in-cheek type of approach, one cannot easily forget the violence of the emasculation and crucifixion scene of John Payne, one of Francis Deacon's friends. In fact, neither the latter nor his friend Ritchie would escape, were it not for a *deus ex machina* type of ending which consists of the unexpected arrival of the hero's father who is going to place the two friends in the office of the District Attorney, thereby saving them from mutilation and death. In addition, the description of Louise Walcott and her cohorts is reminiscent of Vian's virulent pen in *Cantilènes en gelée.* In the poem entitled "Les Mères de Chine," dedicated to Simone de Beauvoir of whose *Deuxième sexe* he had known before the publication date, he wrote in part:

These girls one sees for the first time
They are nothing—one passes by them—
Their eyes are so harsh
And their bodies so tough and darkened by the sun
One feels like making them cry.
They are shut on themselves
On nothing. . . .
One wishes that they cry for a long time
One always hopes that blood would come
After their tears. . . .
But one would have to wait quite a long time
There are only tears
Colorless—warm—useless—
They are like pimples on one's cheek
Pink, swollen, rich with something
You squeeze them—and there is nothing but pus
Insipid—white—useless. . . .
One ought to stick one's sex in them crosswise
So that man on woman
Would be something like a cross
And one could walk on top without fear
One ought to dig into them, empty them
Of this evil of emptiness which they carry. . .
One always hopes to see nothingness cry. . . .
And they remain themselves, tough and cold
And no longer can one make them cry
One must crush them, with masses of cast iron,
Mix together the blood and the bones
Then put the mixture into small cubes
And sell them in a yellow and chocolate-colored paper.[6][7]

Thus Vian's misogyny finds an outlet in a purely aesthetic discharge. But it is difficult to conclude, as does Michel Rybalka,[68] that Vian was no antifeminist, and that his occasional sadism toward women is just one other problem posed by the notion of *the other.* While Existentialism does consider *the other* as evil,[69] and while woman has been defined historically as *another,* Vian himself was no Existentialist, and normally he would pay attention to formulae only for the purpose of mocking them. In the poem just quoted, as in *Elles se rendent pas compte,* however, there appears to be a deep-rooted hatred for the very fabric of womanhood which he considers so beyond repair that only physical dissection and metamorphosis into infinitely smaller and infinitely more insignificant and carefully wrapped parts can alleviate the danger for men that it otherwise constitutes.

And so, while the basic literary validity of *Elles se rendent pas compte* is questionable, for the student of Vian the novel is nevertheless relevant. Indeed, all Sullivan's titles help to explain Vian, to round out and complete his multifaceted complexity. The four books he maintained he translated only contributed in part to his financial stability (at least in the case of *J'irai cracher sur vos tombes*) and, protected to a degree by the partial anonymity of the pseudonym, they allowed him to pursue certain themes, such as sexuality, science fiction, racial and social problems, more than he would have dared otherwise. But, with *Elles se rendent pas compte,* Vian puts Vernon Sullivan to rest, and the former, freed as it were by the latter, can now concentrate his efforts towards the creation of his last two novels, *L'Herbe rouge* and *L'Arrache-coeur,* considered by many as his best attempts at fiction.

VIII   L'Herbe rouge

The fourth novel to be published under Vian's own name appeared originally in 1950 and was reedited following that on a number of occasions, especially since sales increased each time. The two original manuscripts of the narrative bear different titles: "Les Images mortes," "La Tête vide" and "Le Ciel crevé," which the author had considered and subsequently had decided to drop in favor of *L'Herbe rouge.* As will be seen from the summary of the story, each of the above titles might have fit the contents. The book is important not only because it has contributed immensely to Vian's posthumous success, but also because, more than any other story, it is largely autobiographical in that it helps us to understand the causes and the inner workings of the author's actions and reactions.

The main character is called Wolf, a Germanic name for which Vian had opted after his trip to Germany in the summer of 1948. Wolf replaced Ralph, the original appellation of the character in both manuscripts. The story is that of two couples, Wolf and Lil, and Lazuli and Folavril. Wolf and Lazuli, his assistant, have built a machine which permits the main character to travel in time. The purpose of the machine was, initially, that of orienting Wolf into the future, thereby making him escape from the prison of his memories, of his past. However, the contraption he imagined does exactly the contrary, and Wolf is unable to avoid the quicksand of his memories. This, in the end, destroys his marriage too, and results in the hero's suicide.

Nor does the other couple enjoy a happy dénouement. Lazuli and Folavril are passionate lovers, but the man is unable to possess the woman because each time he comes near her, a figure, or a shadow, surges somewhere in the immediate vicinity, and Lazuli's potency is nullified. In vain does he kill the intruder, on occasion, for each time he gets rid of one, another takes his place; and the consummation of love remains impossible even on a sexual level. This is perhaps because, for Vian, in spite of his eccentricities and the apparent divorce in his private life between loftier emotions and sex, love and physical possession remained strongly knotted, indeed inseparable. When social pressures were absent, when he did not have to be or act like a zazou, in the composition of some of his best fiction such as *L'Herbe rouge,* he could have Lazuli tell Folavril that he wanted to possess her "sexually, that is to say with (his) soul." And it is precisely this which is impossible, the communion of the carnal with the spiritual which was envisaged originally by Epicure, but which feeble followers translated into an invitation to debauchery. Lazuli cannot possess Folavril with his soul, hence he cannot possess her. This all or nothing type of approach will tend to contradict the expectations of those who see only the façade of Vian's activities as a Pataphysician. Yet, such an approach is at the very core of his sensitivity as a person and as a writer, prompting him to reconcile irreconcilables: the self and the *other* who, although *another,* is not any more separable from the self than the soul is from the body.[74]

In addition to the unsolvable dilemma of the reconciliation between the flesh and the spirit, notable also is the impossibility of communication between the sexes. This is not only evident in Folavril's vain attempts to excite her lover, but also in the relationship between Wolf and his wife. It will be recalled[71] that Vian had expressed through Wolf the reasons which had led to the breakup of his own marriage. Further explanation, applicable to all couples, is found in the following bit of dialogue between the hero and his wife:

"Place yourself under my skin with me. . . I shall be happy with just the two of us."
"It's not possible," said Wolf. "One cannot place onself under the skin of another except by killing him and peeling it off to take possession of it."
"Peel me," said Lil.

"After," said Wolf, "I shall not have you any more; it shall always be me under someone else's skin."

Thus, communication, understanding, communion, remain out of the question. Women are of no help to men, whether the rapprochement is extralegal such as in the case of lovers, or within prescribed social decorum, as with husbands and wives.

In this context, Angel's affirmation in the later *L'Arrache-coeur* is noteworthy: "Women and men do not live on the same level." Men and sub-women can, however, have a go at the impossible. Indeed, when Wolf and his friend seek refuge in a neighborhood of prostitutes, two of the girls they meet, Héloïse and Aglaé, question the hero on the awakening in him of feelings for the other sex. Wolf is then able to confess, in touching, poetic language, as he would never to his wife, how at age six he had fallen in love with a woman dressed in an evening gown; how he said nothing; how he became aware of sexual desires at age fourteen; how he dreamt of tall women, of Negro women; how the simple act of kissing any of them would play, in his dreams, the role of a most solemn gesture eclipsing intercourse itself; how he checked his desires, invoking pretexts, such as homework, fear of disease; how he realizes now that it was all a question of pride, of fear, and above all pudicity. And he adds: "When I see a woman whom I like, never does the idea occur to me to tell her. For I consider then that if I desire her, someone else must have desired her before me...and I think it is terrible to replace a man who is without doubt just as nice as I am." With prostitutes, however, things are much easier: one never desires them, one simply takes. The world of interrogation, that of problems and dilemmas, is replaced by a purely mechanical one, sensorial but without real pleasure, hardly above that of the vegetable. And once out of it, when the two friends exit tremulously from the prostitutes' neighborhood, questions rise again, and the voids can no longer be filled. In the real world, even the most elaborate attempts of women remain fruitless: "We are pretty," says Folavril, "we try to give them freedom, we try to be as dumb as we must because it's necessary that a woman be dumb, it's a tradition, and, God, is that difficult, we give them our bodies, and we take theirs; and they go away because they are afraid." And to Lil's response that they are not afraid of women, Folavril replies: "That would be too beautiful. Even their fear must come from themselves." The only conclusion is, then: "They are not made for us. They are made for themselves. And we are good for nothing." So, the two women will leave, wondering how they could *take* men for so long, and wishing now "to marry homosexuals with lots of money." Wolf's cadaver remains behind, as does that of Lazuli, and grass begins to grow everywhere, red, as always. Sodom and Gomorrah all over again, inescapable.

The red grass of *L'Herbe rouge* constitutes an appropriate décor for this sinister story in which blood is spilled in a symbolic and a literal sense. In fact, the spilling of the real blood of Wolf and Lazuli follows that of the constant shedding of whatever minute sources of hope there may have preceded. The red grass grows and spreads each time that a disillusionment ousts the possibility of solution. Not only is there nothing one can do for the purpose of reconciling the flesh and the spirit, or the sexes, but even the most imaginative apparatus invented by men fail the inventors and turn against them. Mention has been made already, in the section dealing with *L'Ecume des jours,* that machines imprison and suppress not only the spirit, but even the body of men working with them. In *L'Herbe rouge* Wolf's invention contradicts its purpose and leads the hero on the treacherous path of involuntary memories. Unlike Proust whose aim was to relocate lost time *(Le Temps retrouvé),* Wolf's purpose is to break the bonds of the past and attain the ethereal freedom of the possibility of anticipating the future. This he is utterly unable to do, for the more he experiments with the machine, the more he becomes engulfed in the abyss of his childhood and his youth.

In this abyss an avalanche of recollections falls upon the hero. After awhile, resigned that he is unable to escape, he attempts as best he can to organize his memories. While his efforts do not result in a clear-cut classification, one may distinguish several headings: (1) rapports with family; (2) his life as a student; (3) initial religious experiences, these in addition to descriptions of sexual and marital life already touched upon above, as well as in Chapter I. It goes without saying that Wolf is to a large extent Vian and, as David Noakes remarked, "This novel must have played in the life of Vian an analogous role to that which Wolf makes his machine play. The book has allowed the writer to draw up the balance sheet of his youth. No longer hoping that his novels would attain a numerous public, Vian offered himself the luxury, in *L'Herbe rouge,* to discuss himself almost as if no one were about to listen."[72]

Some of the writer's rapports with his family, especially insofar as his malady was concerned, have been explored already in Chapter 1. But there is more, of interest not only to students of the author, but also to all those who could, in reading about them, identify their own actions and reactions with those of the youngster; for they are not all singular, but rather astonishingly contemporary a quarter of a century later. To be sure, Vian did not say, as Gide did, *Familles, je vous hais!* However, he did decry, as we have seen, his childhood which was too well taken care of, and the showers of attention constantly bestowed upon him. For example, about his parents he says: "They were good, okay, but with bad people one (can) react more violently, and after all this is more profitable." He suggests, then, how easy it is to be good, how it puts one on the defensive for one cannot respond to goodness with violence; hence one must keep the violence within oneself, allow it to prosper and grow out of proportion, like so many cancer cells feeding on themselves and multiplying relentlessly. He describes how, when he was very little, he would visit his parents in the morning, in their bed, and how disagreeable it was to him to watch them kiss each other. How he would go out in the rain wishing that his parents would stop him because he was afraid of getting a cold, and how the joy of going out in spite of his mother's protestations was nullified by the fact that he was nevertheless afraid of aggravating his heart's condition. He tells further that he knew he was soft, that he wanted strongly to vanquish his debility, for which he blamed his parents, but that there were certain advantages in preserving one's frailty. Likewise, in retrospect, he is able to uncover and to dissect thoughts and feelings which in his childhood were only partly conscious but which remained imprinted somewhere in his makeup now unveiled by the machine. For example, the dichotomy between his wish for virility and his softness is one which children of all ages experience, but one which only a genius of introspection such as that of Vian can untangle and clarify. Thus, when describing the *togetherness* of a family picnic, Wolf recalls: "I would walk off in order to have the appearance of being elsewhere, or I would sit at the wheel of the empty automobile, and that gave me a sort of mechanical virility. But all the time, my soft ego would whisper into my ear 'I hope there will be some Russian salad and some ham left.' And then I was ashamed of myself, ashamed of my parents, and I hated them."

Not faring any better than relationships between the sexes, rapports between parents and children are viewed with equal pessimism. They are, after all, not based on love, but on a mutually uncontrollable desire to dominate: domination through the appearance of love on the part of the parents (this love is only an extension of their love for themselves); through sly and unsuspected tricks deceiving their elders on the part of children. The latter, living in a world apart from and parallel to that of parents, have their strength not in their innocence, as usually supposed, but rather in their intelligence which is superior to that of their elders only because the elders fail to recognize it. Thus, there is a fundamental barrier between parents and children, a barrier all the more pathetic since it is one of essential violence under the disguise or the simulation of love. Of course, through Wolf Vian does not mean to intimate that parents and children are, at least in the initial stages, bent on hurting each other deliberately; he merely points out that on the subconscious level reciprocal harm is usually perpetrated and is usually unavoidable. While the naïve might find it profitable to disagree, in order to hold on to their masks, Vian's logic and lucidity are not doubtful for those readers who, unsparing in their own introspection, uncover similar truths.

Wolf's examination of his childhood, dotted with touching, poetic language, is rather mild and passive, however, by comparison to that which he makes of his education and of education in general. To begin with, he views the formal schooling of a child both as punitive and derisory. Punitive because education imposes on the student debatable and changing outside values which, when resisted, are literally forced upon him with violence or the threat of violence; and derisory because the system is so self-centered that it fails to recognize even the most obvious shortcomings which result in its defeat. Upon looking back Wolf admits that he could not bear the contents of the instructional process, nor the atmosphere in which it was administered. Specifically, he accuses his masters "of having taught through their tone and that of their books, that there is a possible immobility of the universe. Of having petrified (my) thoughts at a particular stage. . .and of having made believe that there could be one day, somewhere, an ideal order of things." Such an Aristotelian concept of education was in fact contradicted by the very classroom in which it flourished: "Look. . .at that old desk. Everything concerned with studies is like that. Old things, dirty, full of dust. Paint which peels off. . .lamps full of dust and of fly droppings. Ink everywhere. Holes carved with pocket knives on the desk. . . . And old, idiotic teachers. Spoilers. A spoiling school." Wolf now holds that the self-perpetuation of such a system is only possible because it succeeds in persuading students that doctors, lawyers, engineers (not to be forgotten is the fact that Vian was an engineer) constitute an elite class separate from and above other classes. In retrospect he mocks such an approach because he does not consider himself as part of an elite, because others earn more money than he does and, more importantly, others are happier than he is. And so he explodes: "You know now what I think of your studies. Of your senile decay. Of your propaganda. Of your books. Of your stinking classes and of your masturbating dunces. Of your greenish and glasses-wearing Normalians,[73] of your artificial Polytechnicians[74]...of thieving doctors and of rotten judges...rather a boxing match....It's also phony, but at least it relieves."

Of course, the virulence of such an attack detracts from the many good points it contains. Yet, it must be understood that Vian's revolt addresses itself specifically to the discipline that education requires: the routine of strict hours, the prescribed authors, the confining walls of the instructional plant itself. The alternative that he suggests, a boxing match (elsewhere in the book he opines that it is much easier to learn math than boxing, that it is much more difficult to become a good swimmer than to learn how to write in French) is of course childish, but it should be recalled that it is not the task of the writer or artist to suggest alternatives, that is to say solutions, that when he does, they ought to be passed over quickly if not ignored altogether. Wolf's insistence on such illogical conclusions as: "I hate my studies because there are too many imbeciles who know how to read" (after all, there are imbeciles among boxers and swimmers as well), is not to be taken seriously and should not be allowed to detract from other, more profound and more defensible statements such as:

Do you know...that it is ignoble to impose on children a regularity of habit which lasts for sixteen years? Time is warped...True time is not something mechanical, divided into hours, all equal.... True time is subjective...one carries it in onself.... Getting up at seven every morning, lunching at noon, going to sleep at 9 P.M., and never to have a night all your own, never to know that there is a moment, such as when the sea stops retreating and remains, for a time, still, before high tide again, when night and day intermingle and melt into each other and form a bar of fever similar to that of rivers at the point where they meet the ocean. I was robbed of sixteen years of night.... They made me believe, in junior high, that to get to high school was the only way to progress. After my senior year I had to have my baccalaureate...and then a college degree.... Yes, I thought I had an aim...and I had nothing. I was advancing in a corridor without beginning, without end, in tow of imbeciles, preceding other imbeciles.

These are, after all, anticipatory complaints strangely similar to those one hears today, whether they be voiced at Columbia University or at Nanterre. Vian's ability to condense them in brief, staccato remarks in a novel which is concerned with so many other considerations; his talent for synopsis and terseness with respect to a topic which is nevertheless so close to his sensitivity as a person and as a writer; finally, his painful and sincere awareness of shortcomings against which he rebels but which are, for the most part, unavoidable, point to the singular genius of a personality unafraid, vigorously quarrelsome, impatient, and at the same time refreshing, cheeringly stimulating, and unexpectedly young for a man whose heart condition was keeping him constantly on the threshold of death. When he declares later: "I hated studies because they have worn me out," and still later: "Had I neglected my studies, I would regret their absence as much as I regret now having given them too much of my time," one feels that his mutiny is prompted by the more fundamental problems of man's transitoriness, by the quick decaying process we all undergo, by the very little time left at any stage of one's life, by the misuse of time, and the flight of time, that is, the refusal of nature to grant us eternity.

That death, as Eugène Ionesco was to put it later, "is a mockery and it shouldn't happen to a dog,"[7][5] is also at the root of Vian's adversity toward religion. His interest in theology is even deeper than that in education because the destiny of man always appeared to him to be a farce. The existence of an author of this farce, if admitted, could only enhance the comico-pathetic aspects of it. These, held to be already ludicrous enough, and deplorable enough, do not need the admission of the possibility of a deity which would imply that there is deliberation and order in the cruelties perpetrated on mankind. On the contrary, an anonymous farce is more vulnerable, hence more palatable. That is why, from his early childhood, Wolf recalls, he had had a strong antipathy for religion:

> Father Grille began to laugh.
> "You have a small boy's hatred of religion," he said.
> "You have a small boy's religion," said Wolf.

Although his was an anticlerical family, as a child Wolf-Vian was nevertheless attracted by the mysteries of religion, by his First Communion, for example. He liked to be the center of attention for a while, to go through motions that seemed very serious and very adult. But beyond such superficial considerations there was a desire for an absolute, a sign, a miracle which never occurred: "They get hold of children too early. . . . They catch them at an age when they believe in miracles; they wish to see one; there isn't any, and it is all finished for them." His First Communion, therefore, is reduced to a social event. And later, when he begins to become aware of some of the basic rituals of the Church, he experiences a strong feeling of revulsion: "I have always been embarrassed to see men of my father's age genuflect in front of a little box. I was ashamed for my father." Thus, the ritual is not considered under its symbolic or sacred aspect; rather, it becomes an occasion for a masochistic, self-degrading act. The diminishing process undergone by the believer is shameful and dehumanizing. Witness the lack of coherence, the mumbling, the robot-like utterances to which prayers are reduced, often, in churches: "The chapel was resounding with lambs so sweet, with [words] of glory, of hope and of support! And Wolf was astonished now to see to what point all these words of love and of adoration remained void of significance." In this context one should recall the childish formulae of Father Petitjean in *L'Automne à Pékin*, and the emptiness of the marriage ceremony in *L'Ecume des jours*. Religion is emptiness, Vian held, mystification, and above all inefficiency, as he had suggested in the dialogue between Colin and Jesus in *L'Ecume des jours*. The text of one of Vian's famous songs reads in part:

If I believed in God
I should be happy
To dream of the day when I should see in the sky
An angel in a white dress
On a clear Sunday
Descending towards me in a golden chariot
. . . .
But I have seen too much hate
So much, so much pain
And I know, my brother, that you will need to walk alone
Always trying
To save the love
Which ties you to men of the forgotten earth
. . . .
Thus, my angel,
I seek it in this world
To have finally my share of joy
In its arms.[76]

L'Herbe rouge is, then, a work indispensable to a thorough knowledge of the author. In it he expounds his views on marriage, on the relationship between the sexes, the impossibility of love, and the failure of communication; in it he recalls his childhood, his adolescent years, his lay and religious education, his initial and subsequent reactions as husband and lover. Understandably, therefore, *L'Herbe rouge* has been read assiduously by critics for whom it has provided much revelatory background. Michel Rybalka, for example, noted the degree to which the novel contributed to Vian's posthumous success.[77] Freddy de Vrée lauded the author's ability to reweave commonplace topics such as childhood, education, religion, and marital problems in a real-unreal equilibrium, "somewhere between baroque and simplicity."[78] The latter aspect pleased David Noakes as well,[79] and he further admired the way content and form are wedded in *L'Herbe rouge* so as to result in a truly beautiful and original work. Finally, Jacqueline Piatier, in a newspaper review of the novel, called *L'Herbe rouge* Vian's masterpiece,[80] a narrative worthy of survivial, superior even to the much applauded *L'Arrache-coeur,* the author's last effort at fiction.[81]

IX   L'Arrache-coeur

The last novel to appear in Vian's lifetime was written between 1950 and 1951, and was first submitted to Gallimard, whose editorial board turned it down. In a letter to Ursula Kübler the author commented on Gallimard's refusal, in part as follows: "They are a terrible bunch; I am turned down because I am told that I can do much better things. It's very nice, but imagine [their hypocrisy and also what this does to me]. They all want to finish me. I cannot be angry at them, I know that it is difficult to read; but it is the very fabric [of the novel] which appears to them manufactured. It's funny, when I write jokes, they appear sincere; and when I write something that is true, they think that I am kidding."[82] Subsequently the novel was published by the little-known Editions Vrille. Initially it had no success whatsoever, and Noël Arnaud[83] commented, not without logic, nor without a deep sense of irony and sadness, that it was therefore a masterpiece.

The conception of the story goes back to 1947 when Vian wrote in his unpublished notes: "Novel. Mother and her children, starts by letting them go because when they are small she does not need anything to hold on to them, they return naturally. As their personalities are developed, she imprisons them more and more and will end up locking them in cages. . . . She is like all mothers, her face is beyond description. She ties them, when they are small, with cords which penetrate their flesh. She calls on a doctor to find out how this can be done better." Unlike Wolf's mother of *L'Herbe rouge,* Clémentine is more excessively obsessed by the need to dominate; she is more methodical, a finished monster of a mother who crushes the development and, indeed, squeezes the life out of her three *salopiots.*[84] Little wonder that, when some critics attempted to compare Clémentine to Madame Paul Vian, the latter protested vigorously. On the other hand, in view of the author's constant preoccupation with the relationships between parents and children, it is doubtless that Clémentine's character is partly based on Boris' recollections of his own childhood. The exaggerations in the description of her personality are simply attributable to the usual Vianesque procedures of enlargement and overstatement.

Friends of the writer have determined that the house in which the action of *L'Arrache-coeur* takes place is the vacation home of the Vians at Landemer. There, the paranoiac Clémentine, who has had enough of her husband, Angel, or who is punishing him for her *salopiots,* has locked her mate in one of the rooms. She breast-feeds her children, not without "reticent gestures of mild disgust," deprives herself in all sorts of ways for the sake of her progeny, and goes even so far as to lick their behinds. Her attempts at overprotection are too numerous to mention, but suffice it to point to one as an example: afraid that her children would climb the trees in the garden and fall, she simply has all trees uprooted. Her efforts to place herself on the same level as her *salopiots* in order to understand them better, are equally ludicrous:

"I am going to cry," said Clémentine.
"You don't know how," noted Noël with scorn, suddenly snatched away from his habitual laconism by the truly presumptuous remark of his mother.
"Ah! I don't know how to cry?" said Clémentine.
She burst into tears, but Citroën stopped her immediately.
"No," he said. "You don't know. You go hoohoohoo. While we are going waaah."
"Then waaah," said Clémentine.
"That's not it at all," said Joël.

Mother and children do not exist on the same level, and the only rapports possible are those between warden and prisoners.

The story of Clémentine and her *salopiots* is parallel to that of Jacquemort, a self-styled psychiatrist and friend of the Clémentine-Angel couple. According to Michel Rybalka,[85] Jacquemort is a development of Wolf, a personage who, instead of looking into his own past, immerses himself into those of others through the unsolicited attempts at psychoanalysis in which he engages. "I am empty," he says, corroborating the last syllable in his name. "I only have gestures, reflexes, habits. I wish to fulfill myself. That is why I psychoanalyze people. . . . I do not assimilate. I take away their thoughts, their complexes, their hesitations, and I am left with nothing." Thus, his only desire is to have the desires of others, to be *another,* and of course his efforts are destined only to failure. For example, when he tries to psychoanalyze a servant, Culblanc, the *professional* relationship soon deteriorates into sex; when, in view of his lack of success with human patients, he decides to turn to animals and psychoanalyze a cat, he appropriates the "mental substance" of the Felidae member. Just as Wolf had placed his hopes too high by wishing to anticipate the future, so too his descendant has aspired to an impossible accomplishment. "The one whom I shall psychoanalyze," he had told Angel, "will have to tell me everything. Everything. His most intimate thoughts. His most poignant secrets, his hidden ideas, that which he does not dare confess to himself, everything, everything and the rest also, and even what is behind him. No analyst has done it. I want to see how far one might go. . . . I want to accomplish a sort of identification." Instead of helping patients to discover their own personalities, he wants to adopt theirs; that is, he wants to practice a medicine which does not cure the sick but rather the doctor. Such a medicine, not without its *Moliéresque* origins, diminishes the psychiatrist to the subhuman level of the cat, a fall which is perhaps even more pathetic than Wolf's ultimate suicide.

The collapse of the heroes is due, of course, to ill-placed ambitions. But these would not be needed were it not for the fact that, in Wolf's case, life is simply existence without essence, and search for the latter is both necessary and futile: neither can one go on without trying to search, nor is there anything worthwhile at the end of the always dark and sempiternally malevolent road at one's disposal; the roads which Jacquemort walks when he is not psychoanalyzing anybody are those which lead from Clémentine's house to the neighboring village. To it he makes three trips, each constituting the topic for a short story within the novel, and each on roads just as dim and murky as those traveled by his predecessor.

In the course of the first visit, Jacquemort witnesses an apparently periodic event in town, namely, the sale of old men and old women by relatives to children who use them as toys. The *merchandise* is first showed to prospective buyers, who have the right to examine it before purchase is made. This gives an occasion to the author to point in caustic and sad fashion to the process of decomposition of the old, and to the cruelties of the younger relatives and still younger clients who sell and buy, respectively. The old are dressed in rags, smell bad, and when they are partly or totally undressed by the children, they exhibit their dry, wrinkled, and worn-out flesh. Jacquemort is embarrassed by the spectacle and he questions its *raison d'être* by addressing a man who, on the contrary, enjoys it so much that he cannot stop laughing:

> "Why do you laugh?" he asked, "Doesn't that make you ashamed?"
> The other interrupted him immediately.
> "It doesn't make me what?"
> "Doesn't that make you ashamed?" Jacquemort repeated softly.

He is promptly flattened by his interlocutor's fist, and he learns later that in the village no one has heard of the word shame. While blood drips from his injured mouth, and he lies almost unconscious on the road, the sale continues, and he hears how one of the old men who has a wooden leg attracts a higher price than others. One is intrigued by wooden legs, Vian comments, not many have one, and children like that.

The terseness of the account makes for a very efficient attack on our society's practices vis-à-vis the aged. Not that Vian ever meant to admonish formally the Western world's view of senescence, such as Simone de Beauvoir did many years later;[5][6] his intention was probably limited to pointing in his usual caricaturesque fashion, and through grotesque deformations of persons and events, to the cruelties of the world around us. For indeed, there is only a difference of nuance between relegating the old to petty babysitting activities and their outright sale by parents to children.

In the course of his second visit to the neighboring village, Jacquemort goes to a carpenter from whom he orders two beds, one for two, and another, much wider, for one person. There, an overworked small boy, apprentice of the carpenter, sick from abuse, hunger and fatigue, collapses on the piece of wood on which he is working. His boss attempts to revive him by emptying on him the contents of an old sardine can and, failing, by dumping the entire can down his back. Jacquemort, as during the sale of the aged, is incensed at the treatment of the young. But, when he objects, "You are too brutal," Jacquemort said to the carpenter. "A little boy of that age! You ought to be ashamed," he is again hit in the face and must abandon any thought of administering help.

As in the preceding story, shame is a word that must not be used, a feeling that one must not have if one is to survive. In a universe at whose very core cruelty reigns supreme and provides for the only way of existing, intruders in search of their own essence such as Jacquemort (search by means of efforts at psychoanalysis, attempts to help others) must be eliminated or crushed. Contrary to the views of Existentialists, essence, then, is considered to be a menace to existence: the people in the village, at least those in authority, fare passably well, that is they exist, shameless and remorseless, and therefore find it most impractical to approve of the idea of changing, of remaking themselves into *non-salauds.*

On the occasion of the third visit, Jacquemort meets La Gloire. He is a fisherman of sorts, employed by the village to fish, with his teeth, garbage and other things which the inhabitants throw into the river. He is paid handsomely for his work which is, essentially, that of carrying on his shoulders the shame of the village. When questioned by Jacquemort, he confesses that he cannot spend any of his money because no one will sell anything to him, that in fact, he has only his boat and his house, given to him by his employers. Asked why, in view of the circumstances, he has taken on this job, he confesses that he does not know the reason, nor when he began. He recalls only that another had the job before, and he knows that, when someone else is more ashamed than he is, the position will go automatically to him. La Gloire, then, an enigmatic personage who gives Jacquemort the impression that "he is speaking to someone from another planet," is the collective conscience of the village, performing a task similar to that of Orestes in Sartre's *Les Mouches.* Little does Jacquemort know at the time, or La Gloire suspect, that eventually the former will replace the latter.

Jacquemort's trips to town, like his aborted attempts at psychoanalysis, have helped to make him evolve, to change in certain ways. As in the case of Wolf for whom the machine illuminated the past, Jacquemort's acquaintance with the world around him ends, not in the initially hoped for result, but rather in a retrogression: the hero, instead of acquiring an essence (albeit a derisory one, the essence of his patients), that is, instead of giving to his existence a certain significance which would take him out of the *salauds* category, is forced by the character of his experiences deeper into it. For example, at first embarrassed and revolted by what he sees, he begins, little by little, to join the others and to act like them: he insults, hits, harms, just as often and with as much gusto as everybody else. His backward voyage is not unlike that of Wolf who had anticipated visions of the future, only to become persistently glued to the past.

Jacquemort, who perhaps follows the *if-you-can't-beat-them, join-them* dictum, is further helped in his decision to take La Gloïre's place by the antics of the priest in the village. Like most of Vian's prelates, the clergyman in *L'Arrache-coeur* practices a religion full of pranks and at the antipode of that usually associated with the Church. To begin with, he considers that religion is and ought to be accepted as a luxury. God is a luxury, he says, and only the brutish proletariat attempts to demote Him to a necessity. A Mass which he performs for his parishioners becomes in effect a battle between himself and the attendants. To the believers' cry: "Let it rain," the priest replies: "It shall not rain! God is not utilitarian. God is a birthday present, a free gift, a platinum ingot, a work of art, a light, delicate morsel. Moreover, God is. He is neither for nor against. He is an extra!" When the struggle between devotees and priest reaches the physical point, the latter retracts, and the carpenter explains to Jacquemort: "We let him talk. It doesn't hurt anybody, it's amusing. Here we like Mass quite a bit. With or without a pirest." The ecclesiastic's love for antics of dubious apostolic origin leads him one day to organize a *spectacle de luxe.* As the main feature of the show he fights the devil, that is to say, his sacristan. The battle takes the form of a boxing match, and the priest cheats and wins, to the delight of all spectators who shout: "He is cheating! Long live the priest!" Henri Baudin aptly labeled Vian's view of religion in *L'Arrache-coeur* as "almost Parnassian, a religion-for-art's sake,"[87] that is to say, a matter of decoration and ornamentation appealing to the dandy in us all.

Jacquemort views such a superficial concept of theology as utterly superfluous and derisory; that is to say, that it cannot possibly correct the evil goings-on in town, nor help him in any way. The only solution, then, is that of assuming La Gloïre's role in a supreme gesture of both desperation and resignation. Desperation because he could neither help himself, nor find solace elsewhere; resignation because there is always a point in one's life when the glow of the possibility of an essence stops flickering. At that time, humbled and fatigued, man must abort and give up. Unlike Orestes, Jacquemort takes on La Gloïre's work for no heroic purpose, nor because of any spirit of sacrifice. Unable as a psychoanalyst to have the thoughts or the desires of others, impotent as a traveler in helping those he meets on his way, he is simply reduced to the ignoble task of fishing, with his teeth, the refuse, that is to say, the shame of those around him. Even if he could, in this manner, purchase a conscience, or an essence, the price paid would make the acquisition worthless. In this context it is interesting to note that there is no heart-snatcher in *L'Arrache-coeur*.[88] In the story of Clémentine and her *salopiots,* as well as in that of Jacquemort and of ours, it is obvious that no such device is needed: figuratively and literally, one's heart is always snatched and ultimately stops.

The adulations brought upon *L'Arrache-coeur* have been almost always stated in superlative terms. At the time of its publication, for example, an anonymous reviewer noted that there are in the novel "some extraordinary tableaux. . .and that certain scenes such as the psychoanalysis sessions and the priest's sermon are of the best comicality."[89] Freddy de Vrée stated unequivocally that *"L'Arrache-coeur* is the richest of Boris Vian's novels. . . . The book creates a [whole] climate."[90] Then later he added, *"L'Arrache-coeur* is a greatly profound and mysterious book."[91] According to Pierre Kast, the composition is "a fabulously original"[92] narrative, although David Noakes likened it to the preceding *Vercoquin et le plancton, L'Ecume des jours* and *L'Herbe rouge,* in the sense that they all reflect certain episodes in the life of the author and certain personal attitudes toward life.[93] Both reviewers are correct: the originality of *L'Arrache-coeur* consists in the heretofore untouched comical aspects of psychoanalysis, as well as in some of the very intriguing, if irreverent scenes describing the religious activities in the village; but *L'Arrache-coeur* is also like the preceding novels in that the author continues to persist in his pessimistic outlook on life, in his underlining of its cruelties, and in his refusal to suggest a clear-cut message or resolution. Clémentine, for example, is depicted as a monstrous mother, but her monstrosity is after all prompted by love; religion is seen as utterly inefficient and pretentious, but the populace has fun believing; and Jacquemort is described as a resigned *salaud* at the end of the story, but we cannot forget that he was driven to his demise by circumstances and forces not always in his direct control.

L'Arrache-coeur is the last novel published during Vian's lifetime. In spite of the favor it found with the literary elite, it was not a popular success, and the author gave up future attempts at full-length fiction. He continued, nevertheless, to write for the theatre and to compose and revise short stories.

X Trouble dans les Andains

Vian's first finished novel (he wrote another, "Mort trop tôt," in

1942, in collaboration with his wife; it is an unfinished detective-type story relating an adventure of Le Major) was the last to be published, in 1966, seven years after the death of the author and twenty-three years after its conception.

Trouble dans les Andains, as the back cover of the book informs us, is neither a rough draft nor a primitive version of any of his other works. It is a story of original inspiration, fully finished, written with gaiety and unbridled by anything because it has ripened exclusively by means of the dynamics of words. A direct example of the language-universe of Boris Vian, this is an adventure in which terror (funny), police investigation (caricaturesque), and espionage (James Bond type) intermingle through the words which tie them and sow them, mix them up and solve them. . .and cause one, by their antics, to shake with laughter. . . . A story which Boris Vian had narrated to himself for failure of being able to read it in someone else's book. Yes, a story totally invented, a narrative for pleasure, to amuse oneself, one has the right to, doesn't one?

The editorial enticements herein notwithstanding, *Trouble dans les Andains* is the novel of a youth, something which, happily, can be said of all the works of Boris Vian. Written with unchecked and uncorrected enthusiasm, the narrative tells the nightmarish story of a quest: that of a mysterious talisman which is inexplicably called a *barbarin.* The author never explains what a *barbarin* is, only that two couples, Serafinio and the Count, the bad guys, and Le Major and Antioche, the good guys, go after the talisman. A fifth character, the Baron Visi (anagram of Boris Vian), also searches for the *barbarin.* He is an old man who lives in a cave under Le Major's house. The cave is full of the blood of Jules, a kind of medusa which he has brought with him from some previous trips to faraway lands. The Baron, who winds up being Antioche's father, gives to his son and to Le Major a *precious* manuscript which contains only the expected information that the bad guys are indeed very bad because they are the descendants of the enemies of the Baron. Le Major and Antioche kill them and, with the help of an Indian (for there is also an Indian in the story), Popocatek, they manage to find the *barbarin,* and they promptly kill the Baron for one can never be prudent enough. Antioche reasons the murder as follows: "This way we keep the *barbarin,* and we owe nothing to anyone, and no one knows about it." But at the end of the story they throw the object into the sea. The gratuity of the murder is underscored by the gratuity of the *barbarin,* which itself points to the futility of search. This futility is modified, however, by the fun one has in the course of a quest, especially in the course of a pointless one, which makes the whole adventure worthwhile after all. Of course, all this is somewhat akin to the famous theory of *disponibilité* of André Gide, as youngsters (Vian was twenty-two years old at the time he began to write *Trouble dans les Andains*), and older people, too, chose to misinterpret it.

In his unpublished notes, Vian appears to have regretted, somewhat, the slightly nonsensical episodes in *Trouble dans les Andains:*

I had waited to be twenty-three years old in order to publish. That's a youngster for you. One needs much ambition. Then, I have tried to narrate to people stories which they had never read. Pure stupidity, double stupidity: they like only that which they know already; but I don't find any pleasure in that which I know already of literature. In effect, I was telling these stories to myself. . . . I have only spoken of things that I know absolutely nothing about. That is what is called true intellectual honesty. One cannot betray his subject when one has no subject, or when it isn't real.

His apology, then, becomes a defense, and not a bad one at that. For *Trouble dans les Andains,* whose summary above (or any other) could not do much justice, must be read in order to enjoy adequately the brilliant vertigo of words, the cacophony of sounds, the harmony of sounds, the playful puns, the impossible puns and, in general, all the unlimited ways in which Vian invents words, dissects words, ravages and devastates the dictionary in order to give to it a new and fantastic and unsuspected life. Vian's verbal prolixity is never tiresome or tedious; on the contrary, it lends to what are otherwise superficial James Bond type of activities, serious innuendos which contest reality, transform the certain into the impossible, and the impossible into what is most feasible of all. His use of words as autonomous and as beings independent of their meaning is going to be a procedure very close to his makeup as a writer of fiction, as was pointed out in the analysis of some of his other novels above. But in *Trouble dans les Andains,* perhaps more than in any other subsequent novel, he feels free to throw the concrete into the arms of the abstract, to insinuate the natural under the blanket of the cultural, to play havoc with what is known or expected with the most refreshingly deliberate impudence. Some ten years later he wrote to his friend François Billetdoux: "For me there is no mystery in words. I like to play with them. It's a pity that people are afraid of words: They allow themselves to be dominated by them."[9 4] While his toying with vocabulary forbids translation (only a good knowledge of French, and an excellent knowledge of French idioms can provide a full appreciation of the results), the following example, picked at random, is witness to the subverting manipulation of language of which he is capable:

Physically, he [Le Major] was a handsome, cretinous type, he had a low forehead, hirsute hair, one scowling eye and the other of glass, a satanic grin deforming his thin lips. He took a long time to dress, had all his teeth and professed an immoderate love for a lot of lipstick.

Insofar as his spiritual side, we shall daresay that the lava of a central fire appeared cold next to the boiling furnace of his genial thoughts. But he rarely said what he thought. To conclude, he was a virgin and practiced jujitsu.

As an example of his use of the calembour, it is interesting to note his description of a minor character, Isaac Laquedem, an "ancient poor devil who was reading a translation of the Talmud in green language, because he saw red and suffered from Daltonism."[9][5]

Trouble dans les Andains, then, opens the curtain, as it were, on Vianesque situations and especially on Vianesque language developed usually with more restraint in subsequent novels. Its importance for a fuller understanding of the author is, however, marred by the fact that it was published after all his other fictional works.

XI *Summary*

Boris Vian, then, is not simply the author of *J'irai cracher sur vos tombes.* While Vernon Sullivan wrote novels which gave rise to debate and scandal, the more frequently published Vian did create narratives which are alert, intriguing, full of life, and the love of life, in spite of its shortcomings, and in spite of the specter of death. From *Vercoquin et le plancton* to *L'Arrache-coeur,* one never ceases to be astonished by the author's strange combination of persistent pessimism and lofty laughter. At the same time amusing and disturbing, his novels take the reader into odd locales, into the limitless world of exaggeration and fantasy, into a world recognizable, nevertheless, in which the author's love of freedom pervades, supreme. A passionate enemy of plans and projects, of systems and systematists, his novels represent, perhaps more than anything else, a constant effort to testify in favor of all that which is individualistic, that is, all that one feels directly through his own senses and in his own flesh. Uneven but often brilliant and always contemporary, his full-length fiction is, more than his lesser known short stories and plays, at the basis of the increasing reputation which he enjoys in our day.

CHAPTER 3

The Short Stories

I   Les Fourmis

THE title refers to a volume containing eleven short stories written from 1944 to 1947, some of which appeared first in a number of newspapers and magazines, later collected and published by the Editions du Scorpion in 1949. "Les Fourmis" is also the title of the first short story in the book, the one generally considered superior to and more representative of Vian's ideas and style than the others. It and "Le Rappel" (the latter from a second collection of short stories entitled *Les Lurettes fourrées*) are the only two to be discussed in the present chapter.

According to Michelle Léglise who talked about the details of the composition to Michel Rybalka,[1] in the summer of 1944, the cinemas being closed, the Vians were reduced to going to see, in the *Soldatenkino,* German propaganda films. It appears that our author was so impressed by scenes of the invasion of Normandy that he decided to write a short story on the subject. As such, "Les Fourmis" furnishes Vian with an occasion for an early expression of antimilitarism, a point of view which, as noted in the following chapter, will be emphasized repeatedly in the plays. But before going into a discussion of the story itself, it is interesting to recall that "Les Fourmis," in spite of its anti-*engagement* standpoint, was published in 1946 in Sartre's *Les Temps modernes,* barely two years after Allied forces began their effort for the liberation of France.

The short story takes place in June, 1944, and has as its principal character a young American soldier who, pushed back by repeated German counterattacks, finds himself in a constantly more limited space until, after a short period of remission, he is reduced to total immobility, one foot on a mine which will explode as soon as he moves it. And move it he must because of numberless ants which eat away at the flesh and bones of his toes. The context affords the author an opportunity to launch many humoristic attacks at war in general and soldiers in particular. The anonymous narrator appears to have been tossed on the beaches of Normandy without much training, and without any knowledge of the reasons for the invasion. Robot-like he moves forwards, backwards, stops, moves on again. His sight is hampered by the rainy weather, by the perspiration falling off his forehead, and by the general confusion inherent in similar situations. Bullets fly, grenades and artillery shells explode everywhere, tanks burn, structures collapse, soldiers and civilians die matter-of-factly and promptly stiffen and putrefy.

The narrator is obviously used to such horror scenes for he appears at least spiritually untouched (physically, he first loses two teeth, then two others, which prompts him to conclude that "wars don't do anything for teeth;" subsequently one of his legs becomes injured, but he will have it taken care of by a medic whom he bribes with a bottle of cognac for fear that, in his Hippocratic zest to help, he will cut both his legs off). The astonishments which he experiences once in a while are not prompted by events which are normally surprising; rather they stem from normally intelligible war-like episodes. In fact, the first sentence of the story is characteristic in this context: "We disembarked this morning and we have not been well received, since there was no one on the beach except a bunch of dead guys, or piles of pieces of soldiers, demolished tanks and trucks." Later, refusing to be baffled by the constant downpour which others might have attributed, because of the increased difficulty in moving, to inimical gods, on the contrary, he notes that, "happily, the weather is beginning to clear up, it only rains nine hours out of twelve." Such *optimism* points to the brainwashing procedures undergone by good soldiers, and the author is insistent on this subject for there are numerous other examples in the text which testify to the narrator's refusal to face the inescapable reality of the situation. For instance, he takes delight in learning that "one can expect reinforcements to arrive by air a month from now;" but in the very next sentence he comments without the least hint of revolt: "We have supplies for another three days." And Vian makes this comment particularly emphatic by using it as the last sentence of Chapter VI of the story. Moreover, in Chapter VII, when the planes do indeed begin to drop supplies, they are such that the recipients have little use for them. Later, instead of supplies, parachutists come down, that is, they attempt to, for they carelessly engage in judo fights while in the air, and play at cutting the cords of each other's parachutes. Those on the ground are amused by the show, disappointed when the wind separates the fighters, and once more enthusiastic when the air soldiers begin to shoot at each other. Far from seeing the incongruity of this spectacle, the narrator remarks: "I have rarely seen such good shots."

The period of remission mentioned above is very brief and occupies only a couple of episodes in the course of which the hero tells about dancing with a girl at the Red Cross Center and, on another occasion, taking another girl to a movie. To his astonishment, the first informs him that he is a hero, but he does not comprehend the word and he makes no reply. There is no conversation with the second girl, whom he considers a bit retarded because she objects to his wandering hands. The entire period of remission reveals the boredom of the narrator who, without realizing it, finds combat more spiritually satisfying.

The plot of "Les Fourmis" is dotted with extremely cruel passages in which the narrator describes what he sees without the least feeling of compassion, for others or for himself, violence becoming for him not just a way of life, but also an acceptable, at times enjoyable, mode of survival. When a soldier, upon disembarking, has his face blown apart by a shell, he simply picks up the pieces and puts them in his helmet. With a somewhat modified disdain for normalcy he describes how tanks crush the corpses on the ground, and finally are themselves blown up by mines, so that some vague poetic justice may be adhered to. Of course, in the process, the soldiers who are in the tanks are also killed, some immediately, others trying in vain to escape, their legs inside, burning, the upper part of their bodies outside, riddled by machine gun fire. But even such a spectacle, because it is often repeated, fails to maintain the hero's interest, and he yawns and falls asleep. Swiftlike cynicism and black humor are evident also in the following passage describing an attack with flamethrowers on tanks:

We got hold of a flamethrower; what is annoying about it is that one must first break the turret before making use of the flamethrower, otherwise the turret bursts (like chestnuts) and the guys inside are badly baked. . . . We ended up by getting rid of the third tank with a bazooka which we charged with sneezing powder and those inside hit their heads against the steel so much that only corpses came out. The conductor alone was still a little alive, but his head got caught in the steering wheel and he couldn't take it out; so rather than blow up the tank with which there was nothing wrong, we cut off the guy's head.

A similar effect is produced with a later passage in which the narrator tells us: "Now the planes are returning, I count seventy-two of them. They are not very big planes, but the village is small. . . . I believe that from one end to the other of the village there is not one single house standing. It appears that there aren't any inhabitants either, and those whom we see have a funny look on their faces when they have managed to hold on to them, but they ought to understand that we cannot risk losing soldiers in order to save their homes." And the end of the story reinforces, of course, the author's attack on wars by pointing to the hero's insouciance and inability to assess what is going on: in the last paragraph of the penultimate chapter we learn that he has received a letter from one of the girls he had befriended before, and that two weeks hence he is going to be on furlough, and then in the very first line of the next and final chapter we are told that his foot is on the mine which will ultimately and undoubtedly blow him up.

But in addition to the impassioned attacks on war and violence in the story, Vian manages to make of "Les Fourmis" a particularly appealing exercise in style. The appeal of purely stylistic acrobatics can best be appreciated in the original, and little purpose would be served here by translation of aesthetically pleasing passages. A reading of the French text, however, would reveal the usual Vianesque devices of writing mutually contradictory sentences, in which he inserts apparently senseless but in fact words pregnant with meaning, others partly coarse and partly elliptical, while still others find themselves present for their sound or play value, all revealing his fanciful imagination and showing Creation to be the unreal and absurd complexity that he held it to be. "Les Fourmis," as an early example of Vian's fiction, merits our attention, then, not only because it establishes the author as the antimilitarist he was going to become in later fiction and plays, but also because in it he gives to words a life of their own, in unsuspected, startling, and arresting combinations.

II   Les Lurettes fourrées

Published in 1962, *Les Lurettes fourrées* contains only three short stories: "Le Rappel," which he wrote in 1949, more representative than the others and the only one to be discussed here; "Les Pompiers," composed a year earlier and published in several literary magazines between 1948 and 1962; and "Le Retraité," written also in 1949.

"Le Rappel" relates how an anonymous protagonist climbs to the top of the Empire State Building, checks the direction of the wind by throwing a piece of paper into the abyss below, then jumps. In the course of the fall he looks through the open windows of the offices and apartments that fly by, and fragments of memories are awakened in his mind through associations of words and images. Thus, the reasons which have prompted the suicide are evoked, venial and vague, through bits of recalled conversations and broken interior monologues. As the rapidity of the fall is increased by the gravitational pull, the onrush of memories is accelerated, the real and the fantastic become intermingled, and we are suddenly aware that the irony and the pathos of death are, in fact, the only means we can use in order to escape from the painful banality of terrestrial existence: for the actual plunge into the unknown below is complemented, for the hero, by a concommitant spiritual descent into the past, and the two tumbles result in a heretofore unexperienced awareness of his former existence, of his present aspirations as well, of what death is really like.

Of course, because of his lifelong cardiac insufficiency, Boris Vian went through a not-too-unsimilar slow plunge into death. And, like his maker, the hero of "Le Rappel" tastes, savors, masticates, swallows, and becomes impregnated by the feeling of physical annihilation in the course of his fall. Actually, the fall transforms him and awakens in him a variety of contradictory and complex reactions, colored and reinforced by the bits of memory invading his brain. The recollection of a liaison he may have had with Winnie, for example, makes him realize that he did not love her; and the impossibility of marrying her (because of family problems, perhaps, but facts are never clear in this early example of Aliterary writing) becomes both a reason for suicide and a reason to go on living in order to consummate a desire not yet extinguished. The sight of an infant's room as he tumbles past the floors of the Empire State Building evokes the punishments he suffered at the hands of his mother,[2] and makes him recall how she would put her clothes in his closet because hers was already so full—one serious and one trivial antecedent to his suicide. The smell of freshly-brewed coffee emerging from an open window on the seventeenth floor tickles his taste buds and results in a renewed interest in life, pushing aside, temporarily, the attraction of death, and making him enter, miraculously, the room, where a mystifying conversation ensues between him and the young girl residing or visiting there.

In the episode just mentioned, among the several points debated is that of the similarity of things and situations. The protagonist maintains that what he saw on the way down ranged from the agreeable to the abominable; the girl suggests that everything he saw was alike, that, in fact, had he decided to enter through another window, on another floor, he would have found the same décor, the same tenants, and she too would have been there, for everything and everyone are nowhere and everywhere. He opposes a mild resistance to such a pessimistic view, but is perhaps convinced in the end because when he asks, "What if I remain?" her curt reply is: "You cannot remain. . .it is too late." And so he has nothing left to do but to take the elevator up again and to throw himself once more into the emptiness below, this time, one suspects, without curiosity, eyes shut, until his head "makes a medusa on the Fifth Avenue asphalt."

In spite of the seriousness of the situation, this story is not devoid of humorous passages. In addition to the obvious ones describing the appearance and disappearance of objects and persons in the speed of the plunge, and the fantastic episode relating the stop on the seventeenth floor, there are numerous laughter-provoking allusions, innuendos, and just plain funny, often invented words. For example, the Long Island Virginal style house he mentions seeing in the distance at the beginning of the fall, suggesting the architectural Virginian style and stabbing, through the misused adjective, the lack of innocence of the others, those who live comfortably with themselves, who are not tempted by suicide; his recollection of drinking with Winnie, in a bar, a glass of something called a *petrouscola,* playing on the combination of the title of Stravinsky's ballet, *Petroushka,* and the word *cola,* that common international drink; the evocation of how, during a formal occasion, he found himself, legs naked in his underpants, clad only in a short dinner jacket, and the terrible laughter of those around him; the glimpse he catches in one of the offices of a statue of a horse, and his thought that he prefers Paul Jones, alluding to the white horse on the label of a well-known whiskey, and recalling how he used to calm his nerves with liquor, a palliative that he can no longer consider.

These comic interplays lard through the gravity of the main character's suicidal act. Not only do they provide a necessary humorous relief, but they point to a singular ability on the part of the author to combine the lightest fantasies with the most profound pathos emerging from the threat of death. This ability, already mentioned in the discussion of most of his novels, prevents him from falling into the trap of trite sentimentality. On the contrary, like the procedures used by Louis-Ferdinand Céline and Raymond Queneau, his verbal fireworks deepen the underlying fabric of the story, while at the same time imparting an attitude of consolation and catharsis.

As in most contemporary Aliterature, this narration, written almost a quarter of a century ago, has little thematic link between the episodes recollected and alternating with the sights perceived in the course of the fall. Memories tumble through the mind of the protagonist just as his body does along the façade of the skyscraper. Besides, logical perusal of thought and associations would not have been appropriate to the hero's physical position in space. Moreover, the lack of link plays an even more important role than that of complementing the precarious condition of the protagonist: it creates, supports, and heightens the mood of the catastrophe which is going to end in violent death. The fleeting moments preceding the leap into nothingness, the last spasms of life, become as confused, as alogical as all the years of struggles and defeats which have led to the decision to commit suicide, with this difference, however, that now, the hero no longer has any secrets. While the reader may indeed find the intermittent recollections mysterious, and the unfinished allusions puzzling, the *post-sight* of Vian's character permits him to view the past more clearly than before, to understand perfectly the present, and therefore to nourish only sporadic and vague regrets. That is why he does not oppose the dismissal flung at him by the young woman on the seventeenth floor; that is why he does not hesitate to climb once more to the top of the building and, having seen, having understood in the course of the previous plunge, to dive again without paying any attention to the sights available to him.

The cathartic quality of the narrative emerges from the very ability of the character to repeat his desperate gesture, to accept death as a solution once more, no longer in the heat of passion, but after having been able to view the past again and to contemplate other possibilities (such as remaining on the seventeenth floor, establishing a rapport with his interlocutor, resuming life). The reader, who is not altogether up-to-date with the events leading to the initial gesture, can accept the second with a feeling of detachment, if not one of superiority: for he knows his past, for the most part, or thinks he does, and he is not contemplating, at least not yet, a step similar to the one undertaken by the hero. "Le Rappel," then, is a short story which intrigues and satisfies. It arouses one's curiosity through the oddities it contains, and it rewards through the more advantageously lofty position on which it places, albeit artifically, even the careful scrutinizer of the text.

III   *Summary*

The two titles discussed are generally considered to be the best in Boris Vian's repertory of short stories. The tighter format of the genre, more demanding and more exhaustive of the writer's ability to discipline his otherwise zestful prolificacy, constituted an on-again-off-again happy challenge for the author, as witnessed by the number of short stories he wrote and by his success in placing them in many of the most prestigious French literary magazines. While his contributions in this category of artistic endeavor obviously helped his often precarious financial position, the intrinsic excellence of such compositions as "Les Fourmis" and "Le Rappel" is hardly questionable, for they complement remarkably the preoccupations of his longer fictional works, and of his plays, in a more condensed and aesthetically pleasing mold.

CHAPTER 4

The Theatre

I   *French Theatre Since World War II*

WHILE theatre attendance has diminished in many countries because of such contemporary deterrents as cinema, television, automobiles, and the weekend exodus, in the country of Molière the number of spectators either increased since World War II or remained largely equal to that preceding the War. There are probably many reasons for this phenomenon, but suffice it to recall in this context that, in France, the theatrical tradition is very well entrenched, theatrical groups are often government-sponsored, and the art of dramaturgy is so often and so boldly renewed by French playwrights that interest remains high and box office receipts are, percentage-wise, greater than in most other nations. While some theatrical companies are born and then disappear quickly, most are so enthusiastically supported by the public, prospering both in the capital and outside of it, that one cannot speak of a crisis of the theatre in France as one does with respect to other countries.

Since World War II the renewal of the theatre in France has not been the exclusive domain of the playwrights. Daring stage directors such as Jean-Louis Barrault, Roger Blin, André Reybaz, and Georges Vitaly, to mention only a few, discarded tradition in the staging of their dramatic productions, adopted instead the practices of the "total theatre,"[1] and made the spectator face, directly and without explanation, the conflict on the stage. The authors having already stripped their plays of the *benefits* of story, of exposition, of psychological or social or any other form of analysis, décor was also reduced to a minimum by the *metteurs en scène* mentioned above and, when employed by them, it had little to do with or even contradicted the dialogue of the stage production.

Such procedures caught the imagination of the public, not only that of the usual public in the capital and in the large towns, but also that of the *provinces*. That is why Jean Vilar's *Théâtre National Populaire* became an established institution responding to the most varied tastes with a diversity of plays ranging often from the tragedies of Pierre Corneille to those of Heinrich von Kleist, from the social dramas of Bertholt Brecht to the poetic dramatizations of Henri Pichette.[2] That is why, also, the then budding Anti-Theatre,[3] corresponding on the stage with the movement of the Anti-Novel, of which Vian is considered to be one of the precursors, kept alive the public's interest in spite of the social deterrents alluded to above. The anti-plays, especially of the type that Vian wrote, revitalized the theatre through their depiction of the odd activities and apparent meanderings but really meaning-charged banalities of bored, lonely, extremely depressed and depressing personages. Such a theatre, devoid of tradition, of conformity, and open to all myths, made available new literary vistas to later writers such as Marguerite Duras, Eugène Ionesco, Samuel Beckett, and others, who capitalized on the initial successes of at least some of Vian's plays. In fact, the New Theatre, not so new now any more, can be found, in embryo, not only in the Greek drama and in the *Mystères* of the Middle Ages, but rediscovered and recaptured by our unpredictable author who, as we shall see, helped to unleash once again that ancient form of tragedy in which the danger to characters comes both from the outside and from their very own makeup.

Vian's passage from the novel to the theatre is understandable enough if we keep in mind his constant ability, in the former genre, to make the clichés of daily dialogue pregnant with engaging complexities. His practice of relying mainly on conversation for the development and the diffusion of conflicts in fictional narratives made it easy for him to undertake the more demanding style of dramatic composition. In fact, as early as 1942 he wrote, in collaboration with his wife, Michelle, an unstaged and unpublished play entitled "Notre terre, ici-bas," and *Dossier 12* of the Collège de Pataphysique contains a list of a number of later plays, all unstaged and unpublished, and some unfinished, which preceded his first drama, the topic of the next section.

II L'Equarrissage pour tous

A summary version of the play appeared first in *Les Cahiers de la Pléiade,* Number Four, in the spring of 1948. The magazine, whose director was Jean Paulhan, had been launched (with the catchy advertising phrase, "Long live disengaged literature") in spite of the then-famous Jean-Paul Sartre and his tenets concerning a *littérature engagée*. The editorial article of the first issue commented as follows: *"Les Cahiers de la Pléiade* does not think it necessary to. . .take sides in great social or national conflicts since it hopes simply to air diverse curious texts, modest ones and apparently useless ones, which other magazines and periodicals, busy as they are with grand and noble topics, risk ignoring."[4] For reasons which will become obvious after a discussion of the play, *L'Equarrissage pour tous* fit the motto of the Magazine, which constituted a most daring undertaking in the heyday of Sartre and his followers. Two years later Vian's work appeared in print, and several other editions of it have been published since.

The text is dedicated to Michelle, a dedication which Michel Rybalka finds difficult to explain in view of the fact that the relations between husband and wife were quite precarious at the time.[5] The text's second dedication, however, which states cryptically, "To my close foe: Charlemagne," not only announces the antimilitaristic point of view of the piece, but may also explain the first, for the author probably viewed Michelle also as an intimate enemy. In *L'Equarrissage pour tous,* just as in other works previously discussed, Vian's antimilitarism is especially biting. The story takes place on 6 June 1944 in the town of Arromanches, that is, during the day of the invasion of ·France by Allied Forces in World War II. While bullets fly all around and shells explode closer and closer, a knacker is concerned exclusively with the problem of whether or not he should marry his daughter to a young German with whom she has had a liaison for some four years. Although history is being shaped outside, domestic relations remain prominent inside, and the dichotomy between what is generally considered as grand, noble, and earth-shaking on the one hand, and what is usually viewed as unimportant, even petty, on the other, persists throughout the play and gives it an intriguing flavor that must have displeased many an *engagé* Existentialist.

At the house of the knacker arrive military persons of many nationalities: Germans, Americans, a Soviet female soldier, a Japanese parachutist, and even some French F.F.I.'s. In spite of their apparently different backgrounds, these soldiers are interchangeable. For example, after a game of strip poker, in the course of which the Germans put on the Americans' uniforms and the latter don those of the Germans, it becomes quite natural for the American soldiers to start singing, *Wenn die Soldaten,* and for the Germans to perform cowboy songs. Depersonalized and reduced to bendable puppets as they are, Vian can manipulate them as he sees fit and show warriors as the unimaginative subhumans he holds them to be. For example, the German soldiers' love for discipline is so ridiculed that what would be an asset for a person of another nationality becomes for them a topic worthy only of mockery. The sincerity and idealism of the Americans are counteracted by their description as Puritans, gullible individuals who carry around pre-fabricated clergymen, all of whom are called Robert Taylor. In addition, the Soviet woman spends all her time criticizing the Americans and capitalism, the Japanese commits hara-kiri without telling anybody, indeed and without himself knowing why, the French have been F.F.I.'s only since the morning, and insofar as the British are concerned, they are altogether absent because in those parts one gets off a boat, not on.

At the time when wounds were still fresh and heroes were still remembered, the allusion to the F.F.I.'s and the denigration of the British in the reference to Dunkirk, angered many critics who saw in the play a burlesque at the expense of the brave, equalizing the villain and the virtuous. J. B. Jeener, for example, accused the author of being nothing but a seeker of scandal as a way to fame. He found particularly shocking the remark of one of the personages: "I haven't seen any British," to which another responds, "There is fighting here." And then, quoting Voltaire's famous phrase, he concluded, "It is at this cost that one is *amused* at the Théâtre des Noctambules."[6] In addition, he accused Vian of manufacturing a straw case only, in order to crush it all the more easily, for no one can be said to love wars. A similar attack was voiced also by Mme Elsa Triolet. At the very beginning of a review of *L'Equarrissage pour tous,* she wrote: "I have a solid antipathy for M. Boris Vian because of the ignominy of his expectorations. . . . He takes a sublime era and spits on it."[7] And she went on to say how revolting it was to equate Germans to Americans, and to have the knacker's girl copulate with foes and friends alike, all in an atmosphere charged with the powerful smell emanating from the pit in which the knacker pursues his profession.

Of course, such criticisms are valid only if we admit the introduction of political considerations and the feelings they engender into objective critical opinion. If we do not, we must allow any author the expression of any sort of attack against everyone and everything. On the other hand, it cannot be said that Vian's own aims were apolitical. Attacking the very idea of war and of military establishments is (although the playwright died too early to note it), today, one in vogue with many politicians here and abroad. As he stated in his preface, "War [is] a grotesque obscenity. . .which is why I have tried to take action against it to the limited extent to which anything written and artificial can be effective."[8] Vian, as a precursor of the Anti-Theatre, believed of course in the power of language and in the exclusivity of language. He wrote in *L'Equarrissage pour tous,* for example, about how one ought to rebel against "the absurdity of battles which are battles of words but which kill men of flesh." Since words lead to war, words might also be effective enough to abolish it. Such a conclusion makes of *L'Equarrissage pour tous* a *pièce à thèse* in spite of its vaudevillian aspects, and in spite of the many contrary replies which the writer made to his critics: after all, attacking politics is also the job of politicians, just as writing antiwar plays is the task of belligerent playwrights.

Vian's belligerence is limited, however, by his refusal to fall into the trap of propaganda. In this connection he wrote in his preface: "I have been accused of seeking scandal with *L'Equarrissage pour tous:* nothing could be further from the truth. . . . The play is above all a burlesque: it seemed to me that the best approach to war was to laugh at its expense, a craftier but more effective way of fighting it (though to hell with efficacy anyway). Enough. If I go on like this, people will think I have written something in the nature of 'propaganda for men of good will,' a thought that makes me shudder with horror."[9] That the play is mainly a burlesque can be seen from the drawing and explanation accompanying it on the cover of the original theatre program which depicted a muscled soldier with the head of a horse, and which labeled the play an "anarchist vaudeville." The cover of the program handed out to spectators by the Théâtre Municipal de Lausanne called the play a para-military vaudeville." It appears, then, that the author's political intentions were limited. In a later preface Vian confirmed the limitation as follows: *"L'Equarrissage pour tous*. . .has always seemed to me to be too simple to need explanation. The text had one single aim: to make people laugh about something that is not funny, war. It would have been easy, it seems to me, to lose oneself in the subject by falling into the trap of so-called intelligent thought. I note with pleasure that I did not do it."[10] Then he went on to say that the play is not necessarily an attack against the role of the British in World War II, nor a denigration of the French Resistance Movement, nor an attempt to ridicule heroes. It is simply a farce, he maintained, neither looking for a *succès de scandale,* nor shying away from the possibility of it.

As noted in the previous chapter, Vian had no fear of scandal; at times he even capitalized on it. With *L'Equarrissage pour tous,* however, he found himself in a position more precarious than usual: after all, the play hurt (irrespective of the playwright's intentions) the sensitivities of many, and the author's numerous comments on his work testify to the fact that his defense was at best tenuous. For Vian, no war was justified and no warrior could retain his human qualities. Yet, he was lucid enough to realize that no single farce against war, nor indeed a whole literature of rebellion vis-à-vis conflicts between nations, would ever put a stop to them. And so, at the end of *L'Equarrissage pour tous* war emerges as the victor, for once the insouciance, the laughter, the copulations, the verbal and not so verbal ballets have stopped, a lieutenant arrives, explaining to the knacker that his house is blocking some realignment project of the Ministry of Reconstruction, and must be destroyed. The lieutenant introduces three sappers armed with axes who "are scurrying around shifting furniture and lugging in cases of dynamite," while another officer tries to explain to the knacker the lofty reasons behind the decision of his Ministry: "Now, out there will stretch, in the future, a great vista lined with Japanese poplars. Pleasure gardens and ornamental fountains will enhance the beautiful scene. Flowering plants and bushes will waft their perfume on the breeze." And with usual Vianesque mockery, as the officer talks, the playwright has the sappers light the fuses, whereupon "total blackness descends on the scene, followed by a shattering explosion." When light returns, the spectators can see a backdrop depicting weed-covered ruins, piles of debris in the foreground, and the corpse of the knacker, body separated from head. Viewing this scene, the captain's final remark is "Bah! You can't make an omelet without breaking eggs." He is then shot by the lieutenant, but does not die until after he draws his own revolver and kills his assassin whose last words are: "Long live France!" The strains of the *Marseillaise* are then heard, but the author specifies that it must be played "abominably out of tune," and the curtain falls. The ending of the play points admirably, then, to the ludicrous attempts of politicians to explain and excuse violence in terms of vague, derisory, if not altogether false future benefits. For even if the house does indeed make way for beautiful parks, there is no one left to enjoy them: not the owner of the sacrificed abode, nor even those in authority who have deluded others and themselves with pompous words which hide only poorly their instinctive need of destruction.

Vian has no illusions but that wars will always be with us. His satire of blind nationalism, of reconstruction that is always based on prior destruction, does indeed make one laugh. But the world is such that reaction remains limited to laughter. The latter, then, becomes a means of escape, of survival, for spectators must have a period of respite before returning home to their own domestic conflicts, and/or to the realities of greater ones, those between nations. *L'Equarrissage pour tous* is not bound to make the public go out and demonstrate, or otherwise become actively involved in protest against war, and Vian was not so naïve as to think ever that his play, and subsequent ones which he wrote on similar topics, could ever have such an effect. He knew the role of absurdity in our lives before absurdity became one of the pillars of the Anti-Theatre. He knew the violence within us, also, and like all great writers, he did not pretend to abolish it, he simply opted to laugh at it.

After viewing his drama, one does not blame the knacker for being concerned with petty problems while historic upheavals shape the world outside. As Voltaire had impressed upon us in his *Histoire de Charles XII*, the most eventful events are often the product of chance, and so there is no reason for a father to ignore a very real domestic difficulty and divert his attention elsewhere. The knacker's family, prey to invading military personnel of various nationalities, represents, in spite of the ludicrous profession which the owner of the house exercises, in spite of the loose morals of his daughters, a most human resistance to conquerors who are themselves conquered by the sempiternally blind and oppressive force of nationalism. In this respect, as in so many others pointed to above, Vian anticipated admirably today's widespread vogue against narrow patriotism and selfish, parochial interests. Like Camus, later, in the course of the French-Algerian conflict, our playwright understood that the rights of the individual, even if he be only a knacker, are always pure and always superior to those of the masses. Like Camus who refused to take sides, to defend either the French colonial troops who denied freedom to native Algerians, or to speak on behalf of the latter whose underground tactics were not any less innocent than those of the persecutors, Vian was just as reticent to blame the Germans or to befriend the F.F.I.'s. Militarism is evil in anyone's hands, he thought, and while he died too early to see the end of the colonial era of our civilization, the disturbances in newly-created countries are specific proof of the fact that the violence of the oppressed is just as extreme as that of the oppressors. As Eugène Ionesco was to put it some three decades after Vian wrote his play, nations liberated from the imperialist's yoke have "now as leaders cruel and odious tyrants. In colonial times they lived in poverty, today they live in an atmosphere of terror. Violence goes beyond the needs of violence, because once it is installed, it is greater than the violence which has been dethroned."[1]

Of course, Vian knew nothing of Ionesco at the time he wrote *L'Equarrisage pour tous.* Yet, his anticipation of themes and preoccupations firmly established by Ionesco much later is indeed surprising. In fact, the vitality of Vian's play, as David Noakes noted[1][2] in his examination of it, emerges from procedures strikingly similar to those used by the Roumanian-born playwright. For example, the liveliness of the story springs (as it does in most Ionesco plays) from and is maintained by the constant arrival on and departure from the stage of marionette-like characters who babble a few words and perform a number of pirouettes, appearing and disappearing with equal disdain for logic and chronology. To the resulting chaos is added the confusion of the names of various personages: for example, two of the knacker's daughters are called Marie, as their mother was, a dramatic procedure with which Ionesco was not unfamiliar when he wrote *La Cantatrice chauve* in which all the members of a family are called Bobby Watson. That Ionesco may have been familiar with Vian's work (the King of the Absurd became himself, later, a member of the Collège de Pataphysique) is corroborated by another instance of similarity which exists between *L'Equarrissage pour tous* and *La Leçon,* a play presented on the same bill as *La Cantatrice chauve:* according to the knacker, the number of the license plates of his neighbor's car is "five billion, four hundred-eighty-seven million, six hundred thousand, six zero two;" needless to say, Ionesco, in the course of the arithmetic lesson the teacher gives to his student in *La Leçon,* draws similar comic effect from absurdly long series of numbers.

But more important than specific instances of similarity are Vian's and Ionesco's (and that of other exponents of the Theatre of the Absurd) ability to place their characters below the tragic grandeur of circumstances in which they find themselves, and to point then to their failure to cope with the external events related. The latter, whether they be wars and therefore international in scope, or marriage, and consequently on a domestic level only, remain equally remote from the limited capacities of the puppet-like humans who appear on the stage. In vain Vian wrote in the program for the presentation at the Théâtre des Noctambules: "It [the play] proposes the aim of underlining this truth that a marriage is more interesting than a war, even if it be a world war." For although one cannot find much quarrel with such an assertion, the fact is that, in *L'Equarrissage pour tous,* neither is the problem of violence solved, nor that of the daughter's marriage to her enemy-lover. The answer to no problem can be found, no difficulty can be alleviated, and the abortion of all efforts must always terminate in the physical annihilation of those who try. Vian's pessimism is not diminished even within the contents of a farce.

The potential pessimism of spectators vis-à-vis similarly pathetic riddles is, however, at least temporarily eased by the laughter-causing ingredients of the play. Irrespective of whatever political reasons the author might have had, or of how much he might have offended some, *L'Equarrissage pour tous* accomplishes at least that much. In a very popular song entitled "The Regiment of Ill-loved Ones," for which Vian had written the lyrics, the following lines occur:

> My love goes to war
> With hope flung across his back
> My heart fights like a soldier
> For its happiness in your arms
> My flag is a kiss
> And your smile is my army
> Our love goes forth carelessly
> To victory while it sings.

In viewing his play, as in listening to the words of the song which opposes, in military terminology, love to war, it is quite conceivable that one might be tempted to ignore, for a while, the multifarious reasons for helplessness we find around us. Such temporary catharsis pleased the majority of reviewers, even those who had, because of their orthodoxy in general and their political views in particular, an instinctive aversion for anything stemming from the pen of a Pataphysician. René Barjavel, for example, noted "the boiling burlesque of this 'anarchist vaudeville'. . .the great wave of laughter shaking off the impostors, the fears, the dogmas, all the solemn absurdities in the name of which leaders gather men for flaying and cutting up procedures."[1 3] Likewise, the reputable Mark Beigbeder lauded the comicality of the play, stated that he hoped no one would take offense, and concluded that "it is hygienic to have humor even for what is most sacred."[1 4] Michel Déon, too, remarked that *L'Equarrissage pour tous* is the work of a promising writer whose manipulation of puns, nonsense, and cock-and-bull traits does not make his farce any less serious. "Absurd?" he asked. "I am not certain," he answered. "In order not to have any doubts about it, it should suffice to look at the recent diary of Gide in order to realize that on D-day the illustrious writer read Goethe and discovered that radishes tasted very good indeed."[1 5] From marrying a daughter on D-day to enjoying radishes, there is not indeed much of a road to travel and, if old man Gide found it profitable to ignore history, there is little reason why Vian himself should not have opted for an equal disdain vis-à-vis anything that is not connected directly with one's own individuality. It is precisely this aspect of the play which the reviewer of *L'Aurore* appreciated. He explained: "Threatened as we are by universal and definitive destruction, thanks to the lightning progress of nuclear physics, the objective and integral lumping together of the principals of the recent play, and the demonstration through absurdity of collective suicides can only earn for their author the amused sympathy of future victims of a total and totalitarian war."[16] But it is especially Jean Cocteau who, sharing Vian's proclivities, praised *L'Equarrissage pour tous* more than anyone else. He wrote:

Boris Vian has just given us, in *L'Equarrissage pour tous,* an astonishing play, just as singular in its own confused times as were in theirs *Les Mamelles de Tiresias* by Guillaume Apollinaire and my own *Maries de la tour Eiffel.*
This play, or vocal ballet, is of an exquisite insolence, light, heavy, similar to the syncopated rhythms of which Boris Vian possesses the privilege.
Suddenly, we are in the center of time, at this moment when time no longer exists, when acts lose their logic in the immobile milieu of the cyclone, precisely in that place where the present and the future become tied as one does with two pieces of old string.
And laughter bursts where the bomb bursts, the bomb bursts into laughter, and the respect that one has for catastrophes bursts as well, like a soap bubble.[17]

L'Equarrissage pour tous, then, was not simply a *succès de scandale.* Considering the author's youth and inexperience at the time he wrote the play, it is surprising that he should have been able to weave so adequately, at times even masterfully, his zestful bravado, with regard to any sort of *engagement,* into an equally hearty cluster of humorous situations. As we shall see, Vian's first play augured well for his subsequent theatrical endeavors.

III   Le Dernier des métiers

Written originally because of the brevity of *L'Equarrissage pour tous* and intended for presentation on a double bill with his first play, *Le Dernier des métiers* was nevertheless rejected, because of its highly profanatory tone, by the administration of the Théâtre des

Noctambules and was not presented on the stage until 1964 when it had a modestly successful run at the Café-Théâtre de la Grande Séverine. Using again the device of bitter sarcasm, as he had done in the second dedication of *L'Equarrissage pour tous,* Vian wrote under the title of his second play: "A sketch for Boys' Church Clubs," thereby announcing the anticlerical topic that he was going to treat. The title itself was suggested to the playwright by that of a novel, *Le Dernier des métiers,* written by a friend of his, Jacques-Laurent Bost, and published in 1946. The original edition of Vian's second play appeared first in 1950, in the same volume as *L'Equarrissage pour tous,* and then it was published in a separate volume under the editorship of Jean-Jacques Pauvert in 1965.

The central character is Reverend Father Saureilles, fifty years of age, with a feminine penchant for mirrors, makeup, flowers, and bright-colored clothes. The initial stage directions specify that he is seated in front of a makeup table, much as an actress just prior to going on stage, and that he is surrounded by flower arrangements, calling cards, photos with dedications on them, and all sorts of theatrical posters. Father Saureilles is a proud prima donna, superficial, fat, with an interminable appetite for food and drink, and youthful scouts, ages ten to fifteen, whom he instructs and who constantly surround him. The lessons consist of teaching them to perform B. A.'s *(bonnes actions)* which, when put into practice, reveal the author's aversion not only for the insubstantial teachings of the Church but also for those of any sort of organized group, such as the Boy Scouts. For example, the scouts rush into subway cars, occupy all the empty seats, then show their politeness and respect by relinquishing them to old ladies. They are also good at tying knots, the Peruvian kind, in order to be able to catch grazing llamas, and the Chinese variety in order to be able to repair Chinese sea-going junks.

Even more than the priest in *L'Automne à Pékin,* or the one in *L'Arrache-coeur,* Father Saureilles represents what for Vian is the most despicable fault of organized religion, namely, that of bestowing indulgence on its own prelates. To maintain and foster a high standard of living for themselves first, Vian interjects, the Church needs such satellite organizations as the Boy Scouts, on whose naïveté religion feeds and whom it exploits mercilessly, even to the extent of satisfying the homosexual tendencies of some of its exponents. In addition, other organized groups, such as the police, just as unwittingly aid and rely upon the strength of the Church. When a policeman comes to Father Saureilles and confesses to him his wish to become an actor, our hero delivers to him an apology of the policeman's profession, and ends up asking: "Aren't you the shepherd of bodies, just as I am the shepherd of souls?" And he concludes: "It is noble to devote one's existence to the maintenance of an order which pleases Our Father. . . . Your task is worthy. . .it is humble, because you accomplish your duty without fanfare, without any other reward except the esteem of your superiors, a few bribes, and the satisfaction of seeing Justice triumph on this earth." Whippers of bodies and whippers of souls are all alike, Vian opines, they need each other, support each other, and share in the profits. His denunciation of the nefarious alliance between the Church and the Police is one which is as old as the Church itself, but his revival of it is nevertheless refreshing and stimulating because he states it both with extreme vigor and engaging humor.

Another example of humor which literati in particular, but also the general public, cannot help but enjoy is Vian's reference to Paul Claudel in *Le Dernier des métiers.* In it he has one personage, Paul Quelaudel, famous author of the *Complet de Sapin,* of *Père Aplati* and of *Répartition Méridienne,* [18] send to Father Saureilles, in spite of his "well-knwon avarice," and as a sign of friendship, a huge funerary bouquet. Nor can those who approach the play without preconceived notions fail to take delight (being shocked by a description does not preclude enjoyment thereof) in Vian's portrayal of Jonas, the sacristan. In the author's words, he is "a nice old lady," who throughout the play knits an immense and interminable sock. The sock represents his B. A., a task which he has been performing since he was a youngster, interrupted only now and then by his main duty which is that of dressing, undressing, combing the tresses for, and otherwise playing the role of a *femme de chambre* for Father Saureilles.

Such virulent anticlericalism is reminiscent of Vian's famous radio broadcast organized by the chorale of the *Saint-Germain-des-Pieds,* of which he was a member. His speech was taped and transmitted by some Belgian and Swiss radio stations in 1947. The broadcast opened with a preface by Le Major who set the stage in the following words: "Pimps! Sons of bitches!" Whereupon a frightened speaker announced that the French Radio Diffusion Company had been taken over by rebels and Boris Vian was named by them as General Director. In the course of the news bulletin which followed, containing a variety of puns at the expense of all sorts of established authorities, the following anti-Papal arrow was launched:

SPEAKERINE: Vatican City.
VOICE: Last night, the Pope's wife rebelled, sirs. She asked for her

right to divorce, sirs. But, since to do it she needs the permission of the Holy Father, sirs, it is quite probable that she will never obtain it.

Later in the course of the broadcast, an author and a censor converse on what one may and may not include in a radio program, and an allusion is made to the St. Bartholomew massacre, allusion which obviously could not please the generally Catholic and conservative French audiences which had tuned in. It is interesting to know that a year later, in 1948, Vian pursued what was for him one of his favorite targets, namely, Mother Church, by attacking at the same time Father Army (much as in *Le Dernier des métiers* he was going to attack the brutish force of the Police and the more subtle, although not less violent strength of the Church). In one of his "Chronique du menteur" columns for *Les Temps modernes,* he devised seven different ways of disposing of a general (the latter had to be destroyed because in the author's views the plural of *un général* was *des générés*). The seventh and final prescription of eradication was "to send him a vision and to let him become King of the Carmelites or Emperor of the Jesuits."[19] This may not help, however, Vian stated in the same context, because the Pope might send him a dispensation from ecclesiastical service if he agreed to drop a bomb on a neighboring country.

Vian's wit in such passages constituted an appropriate background for the slingshots in *Le Dernier des métiers.* Indeed, Father Saureilles seems to be the most despicable of the author's priests. He is a character who bears the brunt of Vian's aversion for the Establishment, an aversion which was all the more acute at the time he wrote the play, in view of the difficulties he was having with *J'irai cracher sur vos tombes.* Unlike his other prelates, the hero of *Le Dernier des métiers* is not only inwardly violent and subtly malicious, aspects which the author bestowed upon other characters wearing the cloth, but he is also deprived of that quality of virility with which the others had been compensated. His appetites are limited by his feminine tendencies, just as his intelligence shines only within the confines of a group of teenagers, a perhaps lunatic policeman, and an effeminate sacristan. Given the brevity of the play, Father Saureilles lacks the gradations and the nuances in the make-up of Vian's other priests. This is an aspect which Michel Rybalka criticized in his very brief account of the sketch,[20] one which made even a friend, Freddy de Vrée, ironically label the play a "short sketch in good taste," adding however, "but not too good."[21] On the other hand, reviewers of the 1964 production were almost unanimous in their praise of the healthy laughter it provoked, and the typically Gaulish zest of the author. David Noakes's remarks may be said to summarize those of other critics when he declared: "One understands that not everyone can be pleased by a juxtaposition of a typically Boy Scout mentality and a radically anticlerical priest [that is, one who could give rise to or help maintain an already existent anticlericalism], but the play could well provoke the hilarity of an unsuspecting and sporting public."[22] *Le Dernier des métiers,* then, is not simply an amusing little sketch, it is a boisterously funny, arousing missile fired at one of Vian's favorite objects of derision.

IV   Les Bâtisseurs d'Empire

The dramatist's third play was written in 1957 and appeared in *Dossier 6* of the Collège de Pataphysique on 29 gueles 6 (23 February 1959). It was reprinted in the *Collection du Répertoire* of the T.N.P. in 1959, on the occasion of its presentation by the Théâtre National Populaire under its famous then-director Jean Vilar. Several other editions have been published since, and the play was incorporated in Vian's *Théâtre.* Moreover, and attesting to its popularity, two school printings of the play have appeared in this country: one by Macmillan in 1966, entitled *Deux pièces sur la fin d'un monde* and including also Jules Superveille's *La Belle au bois,* and another published by Appleton-Century-Crofts in 1967, under the title *Panorama du théâtre nouveau,* Volume III. *Les Bâttisseurs d'Empire* is also Vian's play which saw more translations than any other. Among the languages in which it was presented are Swedish, Dutch, Italian, German, besides English, and it was generally well received when it was shown on the stage in England and in the United States.

The author's original idea appears to have been that of writing a novel which he was going to entitle "Les Assiégés." The theme was going to be that concerning a child who is under house arrest, such as Zénobie is in *Les Bâtisseurs d'Empire,* and one which is exploited also in *L'Arrache-coeur.* In an unpublished note Vian wrote: "Everything will take place in the house. They receive a letter and they move to a floor above." Later Vian abandoned the idea of writing a novel, replaced that of the letter with The Noise (more of which later), and invented the character of Schmürz.

The word "Schmürz" has quite a history behind it. It appears that it was Ursula Kübler who invented it in 1957, in order to designate something or someone contradictory of one's wishes. The word began to be used frequently in the Vian household in such expressions as

Schmürz alors, Il est bien schmürz, ce type-là, and *Schmürzerie.*
Linguistically, "Schmürz" derives probably from the German *Schmerz,*
meaning pain, and *Schmutz,* signifying dirt. The sound of the word
must have pleased Vian more than its derivations, for he employed it in
a variety of ways in a number of works: there is a town called
Schmoutz in a radio sketch entitled "Elsa Poppins," a Doctor Schmürz
in a review published in January, 1958, in the magazine *Constellation,*
an orchestra leader called Schmürtzwangler in *En avant la zizique,* and
the author himself adopted the pseudonym of Adolphe Schmürz for a
number of articles which appeared in *Constellation* from June to
August, 1959. In the play under discussion, the Schmürz is a sort of
antiperson, a character dressed in rags whom everyone mistreats,
everyone, that is, with the exception of Zénobie. He is perhaps a
double of the Father, an unbearable presence whom Father and Mother
hit, throw about, torture, eventually shoot, and who refuses to die. In
Freddy de Vrées's interpretation, "the Schmürz was a Schmürz;"[23] and
then he went on to explain: "Schmürz does not mean freedom, malady,
fear, Boris Vian, God, youth. . .but rather what is *meaningless,"*[24] in
one's life and/or in the world. In fact, the conservative critic
Jean-Jacques Gautier, for whom Vian had very little use (in the play
itself there is a certain Jean-Louis Gautier, cousin of the Father and a
student of medicine whose mental agility is described as quite reduced;
in *En avant la zizique* the critic is even more directly attacked and is
labeled as one with "an inferior mental structure"[25]) and who had very
little use for avant-garde writing, was pleasantly surprised by the character
of the Schmürz and wrote an astonishingly good review of the play
because of it:

A point of detail amused me and reassured me on my limits.
In the three acts there was a dumb personage, a kind of monster
wrapped in bandages and enormous slabs of foam rubber. As they were
passing by, everyone (with the exception of the daughter) kicked him.
At the end, he appears to stifle the loquacious man (the Father), the
solemn imbecile, the falsely courageous one now left alone. He appears
in fact to die soon with him. We are told nothing about this personage.
Guessing is quite in vogue in today's theatre. I was wasting my time in
conjectures, not without shame for my little aptitude in solving this
kind of riddle. And I did not dare tell anyone that none of my
hypotheses "fit" all the characteristics of the bibendum in
question. . . . And I knew (then) that I would no longer be embarrassed
when incapable of solving such enigmas. The fan of contradictory
certitudes [those given to him by friends whom he questioned on the

meaning of the Schmürz] has cured me of a great inferiority complex.[26] In retrospect, there is little wonder, then, that some of those who saw the play in 1959 took the Schmürz to be an Arab because France was in the middle of the Algerian crisis, while others saw in him a North Vietnamese because in 1959 the newspapers were filled with news items relating to Southeast Asia, while still others (the director of the play in Stockholm) depicted him as an oppressed Negro.

The story of *Les Bâtisseurs d'Empire,* whatever there is of it, is limited to events occurring to a small family: Father, Mother, and daughter, Zénobie. As the curtain opens, in the semidarkness of the stage, amid shouted directions, noisy stumblings and obvious confusion, a family spills out of the stairway, dropping luggage and household possessions all over the room, and collapsing in relief. Whatever the dreaded, encroaching danger was, it must have been really close because the characters are literally terrified. As the lights invade the stage and we see the frozen poses of the members of the family, an unbearable Noise fills the theatre, yet Zénobie is the only one to acknowledge it. It appears that The Noise is what had chased them away from their previous apartment, and from the one before that, and from several others in the past. It is also suggested that each time the family has moved, one or more members disappeared, and each time the apartment selected was smaller and poorer than the one before.

While the characters converse about the past and the present, in meaningless chatter that sheds little light on the situation, The Noise becomes increasingly strident and nerve-racking. Mother's and Father's refusal to admit the presence of The Noise and its danger parallels their *acceptance* of the Schmürz whose existence they need as a target for their frustrations. Likewise, Zénobie's acquiescence to The Noise complements her vaguely stated pity for the Schmürz whom she refuses to kick, whip, stab, slap, and knee in the groin, as her parents avidly do, without comment or provocation. Another difference between daughter and parents emerges from the fact that the former does not shy away from reality (she realizes that members of the family have disappeared, that the rooms have shrunk, and their possessions have diminished), while the latter deny that there was any change, and attempt to convince Zénobie that she is not in fact cooped up, and that there are no dangers to explain because there are no explanations. Some things there are, however: there is the teasing and the torturing of the Schmürz, a palliative not to be sneezed at; there are the lists of synonyms and antonyms which constitute almost entirely the speeches of the Maid, speeches which not only reassure the perhaps demented orator, but also amuse her listeners; and there is, above all, a possibility of ignoring what is happening by dwelling in the past. When a Neighbor mysteriously appears, the following characteristically trivial retrogression occurs:

NEIGHBOR: Yes, children are astonishing these days.
FATHER *(intrigued):* What do you mean by that?
NEIGHBOR: Well, before, isn't that so, they were quite different.
MOTHER *(convinced):* You are right indeed.
ZÉNOBIE: Before they were different in what way? You were the ones who were children before. So! How can you compare?
NEIGHBOR: You're stuck there with a daughter who thinks much, it's plain.
FATHER: Don't you see, Zénobie, you must understand that comparisons may take place in time [that is, that they may make time pass]?
ZÉNOBIE: But then who compares? You cannot compare now, you with your idiotic mentality, the child that you were long ago with the young girl that I am at present.

The daughter's protestations and her repeated attempts to make her parents see what is going on notwithstanding, the others persist in their incursions into the past. Their recollections are not only meaningless in terms of the present, but are derisory in themselves. For example, Mother and Father talk about how they got married in church, about the mayor of their town who was a homosexual. What counts are not the events recalled, but the fact that conversation on them permits time to pass more easily by allowing the speakers to dabble in quasi-symphonic variations on unchangeable themes. Towards the end of the play, in fact, Father asks himself: "I wonder if I am not about to be playing with words. And what if words were made for that?" If the answer to this question is in the affirmative, then passages such as the following one become acceptable not only because of their burlesque quality, but also as an example of crutches at the disposal of those of us who are, like the characters in the play, subject to constant and unspecified dangers: "I have let my beard grow in order to see why one lets his beard grow. And I wound up with nothing but the beard. The beard is the reason for the beard." These are, of course, Ionesco-like paralogisms, and it may be that Henri Baudin was correct when he advanced the uncorroborated opinion that Vian wrote *Les Bâtisseurs d'Empire* "as a friendly challenge to Ionesco."[27]

In the end, as personages sometimes vanish in Ionesco plays,

Zénobie, Mother, and Maid disappear as the family disintegrates in the face of Noise's assault. Father is left alone, with no one to listen to his chatter, no one but the Schmürz, that is, whose body remains immune to words, fists, and bullets alike. Deprived of the audience required for the dialogue-monologue in which he had engaged before, he now begins to pay attention to the objects around him. The derisory objects left become, despite their paucity and poverty, the only proof that behind words there is something, that words represent something after all, something vague, remote and controversial, but something nevertheless. For example, there is a box on the chimney, a gun, a shirt he used to wear, an old officer's uniform which perhaps used to be his. So he puts on this uniform, and in the course of the monologue which ends the play he boasts that he has become an old man "not without having, like all free individuals, an attachment for this invisible but palpable entity, intangible but, oh, how vital, that one agrees to call the Fatherland, even though, in foreign languages, it has another name." And he continues, in spite of the fact that one of his last gestures is to put on an officer's uniform, in what are, or what he thinks are antimilitaristic terms:

An enemy dressed as a military person is twice an enemy for an antimilitarist. Because an antimilitarist has, nevertheless, national sentiments, and he seeks, therefore, to bring harm to the enemy of his nation. Or, what better way if this enemy is dressed in a uniform, than to oppose to him another uniformed person? It follows from the preceding that every antimilitarist has the duty to enter the army and, in so doing, he accomplishes three exploits: first, he irritates the enemy soldiers; in addition, he annoys, in his own country, the soldier of another armed service, a uniform having as one of its interesting aspects that different uniforms detest each other; also, he transforms himself into an element of an army which he abominates and which, therefore, will be an inefficient army. For an antimilitarist army carries its own cancer and could not oppose itself to a true army composed of private patriots.

Thus, Vian, who had already ended *L'Equarrissage pour tous* on the sarcastic notes of a derisory *Marseillaise,* and who will follow the same procedure at the end of *Le Goûter des généraux,* continued to exploit in the present play as well the comic possibilities of ultrapatriotic sentiments. And, at the very end, as befits his rhino character, he has Father jump out the window while the stage directions specify that a bunch of Schmürzes, "perhaps," invade the stage.

Like the villagers in *L'Arrache-coeur* who refused to pronounce the word *shame,* Father denied the presence of The Noise in spite of the ravages it caused in his household and his family. His *bad faith* merited the evanescence of his wife and daughter, of his maid, of most of his possessions, and ultimately of himself. Those who refuse to stare back into the face of the Absurd, Vian suggests, cannot have any other fate.

In 1959 the theatrical public was ripe for such a conclusion, as evidenced in the universal success of Ionesco's *Rhinocéros* a year later. While Vian's play did not attain the fame of that of the *Roi de L'Absurde,* it nevertheless corroborated and enhanced his position among contemporary playwrights. Reviews were, almost without exception, more laudatory than ever before. Martin Esslin, for example, commented: "How Boris Vian would have laughed about the reception of his last play in London! The solemn and somewhat pained, but totally purblind attempt at analyzing what the establishment critics regarded as symbolism in this play, the delightful mixture of ignorance and arrogance with which closed minds are apt to confront a genuine work of the imagination that does not fit into any of their categories."[28] The *ignorance and arrogance* mentioned by Martin Esslin referred to a small number of very scant and very unimaginative reviews of some second-rate British critics for whom anything that smacked even remotely of avant-garde writing remained suspicious. He might have had in mind Philip Hope-Wallace, for example, who labeled *Les Bâtisseurs d'Empire* an "Intellectual grand guignol;"[29] or Roger Gellert who took to task the Pataphysical aspects of the play and commented: "It is the style rather than the subject matter of the school (in which, by the way, I don't include Beckett *(sic)*) that I find so depressing;"[30] and Laurence Kitchin, whose review was ironically entitled "Vague Symbols from the Left Bank,"[31] but who, according to Martin Esslin,[32] upon seeing the play once again, changed his mind, too late to modify his written opinion, however, because of his paper's rigid deadline.

Most other reviewers corroborated subsequently the initial impression of Martin Esslin. David Noakes, for example, mentioned the "extraordinary impression produced by *Les Bâtisseurs d'Empire,"* and concluded that "It is almost entirely due to *Les Bâtisseurs d'Empire* that Vian owes his reputation as playwright. . . . The play is worthy of the success that it continues to have."[33] Likewise, Henri Baudin confirmed the value of the play which, in his opinion, launched in 1959 the posthumous existence of the author.[34] What these critics, and many others, hailed was the fact that this drama of the Absurd, written in only a few days, is in fact a masterpiece of humor and tragedy, moving and surpassing the personal obsessions of the dramatist who, in other plays, had alienated many because of his haranguing about his two pet peeves: clericalism and militarism. In *Les Bâtisseurs d'Empire,* on the contrary, there is less emphasis on strictly personal preoccupations and the author espouses instead those marring the existence of all men living under the threat of pain and death, much as he has done in his more successful novels. In addition, the play's success with the European intelligentsia was due, in part, to its many affinities with other examples of Anti-Theatre, and with a number of literary currents preceding and following its composition. For example, Mother's and Father's lack of memory can be linked to similar defects of characters in plays of Beckett and Arrabal as well as novels and plays of Marguerite Duras. In contemporary literature defective memory is indeed a frequent trait of personages, pointing at once to their innocence and to their physical and spiritual decomposition. Moreover, the associations of *Les Bâtisseurs d'Empire* with the Existentialist movement have already been mentioned. Also, the Maid's semisymphonic variations on words and, in general, the characters' persistence in illogical conversational pursuits, are reminiscent of a host of contemporary writers and works, those of Beckett and Ionesco in particular. In fact, her accumulation of synonyms and antonyms in numerous senseless speeches is a dizzying and laugh-provoking device reminiscent of the *fabliaux* of the Middle Ages and of Rabelais. The frequent literal interpretations of idiomatic expressions in *Les Bâtisseurs d'Empire* is, also, a device used by such famous twentieth-century writers of farce as Georges Feydeau, and brilliantly exploited by many other playwrights. The distortion, misuse, or overuse of clichés likewise point to familiar dramatic procedures and add to the humor of the play. Finally, the scene in Act II in which Father mimics his *aventure* (the story of his life) can be compared to the dream sequence in the second act of Ionesco's *Amédée ou comment s'en débarrasser,* to the first tableau of Jacques Audiberti's *Quoat-Quoat,* and to many similar scenes in the plays of Beckett.

In summary, it may be said that two main reasons stand solidly behind the success of *Les Bâtisseurs d'Empire:* Vian's exploitation of comic techniques which, far from rendering the human condition palatable, enhances and maximizes the tragedy of characters caught between an invisible Noise and a visible Schmürz and, secondly, the author's deft incorporation into his story of themes and currents so contemporary and so in public demand.

V   Le Goûter des généraux

Written before *Les Bâtisseurs d'Empire,* but published only in 1962
and presented on the stage for the first time in 1965, *Le Goûter des
généraux* is another of those Pataphysical compositions which mocks
effectively patriotism and militarism. The first manuscript of the play,
which is in many respects different from the second and final one, dates
from 1951, and the general idea of the plot seems to have come to the
author while he was working on a translation of General Omar M.
Bradley's *A Soldier's Story.* The revised and final version was published
by the Collège de Pataphysique on 4 Clinamen LXXXIX (26 March
1962). The play is preceded by an introduction signed "Latis" and
entitled *"Actualité du Goûter des généraux,"* of which a significant
excerpt is the following: "Nothing is more general than the General.
And we don't think that we are abusing the complaisance of the deceased
by supposing that, thinking of the motto of the Collège, he would say
with Aristotle and with us that 'the thing to do is to go from the particular
to the General.' " While puns of this type lose a great deal in translation, it
may be interesting, nevertheless, to know that those in charge of the
publication at the Collège de Pataphysique constituted what was called
the *Sous-commission des Ersatz.* Various other editions of the play
were published subsequently, and noteworthy is the English translation
under the title *The General's Tea Party.*

   Le Goûter des généraux is one of the longest among Vian's published
and unpublished dramatic repertory. In Act I, James Audubon Wilson
receives from the government the order to start a war because the
country is suffering from a crisis of over-production. At first he resists
because his friend, Lenvers de Laveste, says: "Oh, it's very disagreeable,
you know, nothing disorganizes an army like a war." Later he agrees,
however, because orders are not questionable, and he invites a few of
his general friends to a tea party at his mother's house. A great deal of
discussion takes place between them on various details requiring
attention, although it is only at the end of the first act that Audubon
Wilson recalls, but without any astonishment. that he was not told
against what country or countries he was supposed to prepare to fight.

   In Act II, Léon Plantin, President, calls into his office three generals:
the American Jackson, the Russian Korkiloff, and the Chinese
Ching-Ping-Ting. In vain he tries to persuade them of the necessity of a
war, for no one wishes to fight France. In fact, Ching declares seriously
(Vian never hesitated to poke fun at Gaulle-ish visions of grandeur):
"You are a country sufficiently glorious to find an enemy all by

yourselves!'" But it is he who proposes a solution, namely that France should fight Morocco and Algeria.

The third act takes place two years later, in a shelter forty meters underground, somewhere in Sweden. There we find Plantin, a Monsignor called humorously enough Tapecul, and all the generals with the exception of Jackson. The news emanating from the war is so good that they can think only of amusement, and so they begin to play Russian roulette. Each drinks, sings, and shoots himself very matter-of-factly, then dies amid the burst of laughter from the survivors. Near the end only two generals are left: Audubon Wilson and one of his friends, called Dupont. The hero finds the game of Russian roulette so intriguing and so enjoyable that he says at one point: "Oh, how super! Let me try! *(He loads the weapon and twirls the cylinder.)* One...two...*(Pulls the trigger. Nothing happens.)* Damn! Lost! *(He twirls again, pulls the trigger, the gun fires and a picture drops off the wall.)* Ha! Nearly! *(He tries a third time, the gun goes off and he drops dead, crying out):* I have won!'" Whereupon

A thin, small sound suddenly swells up: it is the "Marseillaise" *being played on a reed pipe. Enter Dupont, dressed in full ceremonial uniform, his saber at the slope, drawing behind him a small cannon on wheels. He crosses the stage singing:*
March on. March on.
March on, march on, march on.
Let's march with heads aloft.
Along a road that's soft.
March on. March on.

The comicality of this play springs mainly from the fact that all the characters are puppets whom the author can manipulate at will for the purpose of showing how the burlesque of their attitudes underscores the danger which they represent. In a country in which the gross national product grows uncontrolled, the army is looked upon as a means of absorbing and using the surplus, for "it is the consumer who pays the army...and it is the army which consumes." Moreover, Vian refuses to take sides in the struggle between the big powers: he introduces in the same room and places equal emphasis on the derision of American, Russian, Chinese, and French military delegates. The chatter, contradictions, and evident puerility of the characters mix incongruously with their opportunism and their absolute selfishness. The obvious conclusion is that what the spectator faces are not organized, austere and disciplined generals, but rather a group of children playing a game of war. For example, the general in command of all the others, the one who has the highest responsibilities, James Audubon Wilson, does not dare invite his comrades to an afternoon tea without obtaining permission from his mother first. In addition, the very fact that generals gather to discuss mobilization procedures while sipping tea and munching on dainty goodies destroys the virility one usually attaches to their profession. But it is especially the initial scene of the play, with its hilarious dialogue between mother and General-child that sets the tone for the entire production, and points to Vian's ability to combine successfully his antimilitarism with his already frequently stated dislike for assiduous, motherly attention (much as he has done in *L'Herbe rouge,* in *L'Arrache-coeur,* and in other works):

AUDUBON: Oh, drat it! Mama! Mama! Oh, I'm absolutely furious! *Mama!*

MOTHER *Voice offstage):* What is it *now,* you naughty boy? *(She appears: she is a repulsive creature, dignified, white-haired.)* What is the matter?

AUDUBON: Oh! It's so exasperating. It's this tie. I just can't get the knot tied.

MOTHER: Come now, Audubon, don't get excited. You only have to ask mama.

AUDUBON: Oh! I just can't bear things resisting me like that! It's so humiliating!

MOTHER: No, no, Audubon, there is nothing humiliating about it. This is mere manual work, whereas you were created to think, to reflect, not to use your hands like any clodhopper.

AUDUBON: But I am a general, mother. . .

MOTHER: Yes, indeed, and the brain of your body of troops.

AUDUBON: Not "body," mama, "corps." In my case, "army corps." A full general commands an army corps, a brigadier general commands a brigade, and a lieutenant general commands a division.

MOTHER *(Knotting his tie):* Ah, well, Audubon, as your late father always told you, in your army corps you must be the brain which commands and which is always obeyed smoothly by your organization's innumerable cogwheels, by virtue of the soothing and mollifying oil which constitutes discipline. There, look how nicely I've tied your tie.

AUDUBON *(Kisses her hand):* Mother, you're an absolute darling.

MOTHER: Ah, Audubon, if it wasn't for me you'd fly into a tantrum twenty times a day. Now, have you washed your feet well?

AUDUBON: Yes, of course I have, mother.

MOTHER: And your ears, too? *(Audubon nods* "Yes.") Well, I'm going to have a look, Audubon, to make sure. I remember very well what a struggle it was trying to clean your ears when you were six years old. *(She inspects them.)* Hmm. This ear looks a bit dubious, my boy.

AUDUBON: Oh! You can't have looked properly, mama. I'll show you. *(He picks up the towel and proffers it to her by one corner. She studies it, nods her head and puts it back.)*

MOTHER: That's a good boy. Ah, Audubon, how sweet your little ears were when you were tiny. But here you are now, a great big grown-up military booby getting into even worse scrapes than when you were a little boy and dipped the kitten into the soup to give her extra energy. *(She laughs. He sulks.)*[3 5]

The spectator can overlook the lack of verisimilitude of such a scene, as well as the numerous exaggerations in the others which follow, in favor of the effervescent mirth sparkling throughout the play. In this connection, Audubon's formula for national unity deserves mention: "In a word, Work, Family, Fatherland, Honor to the Unknown Soldier and to the dead of the Valerian Mountain, and all of us behind the tricolored flag." Each time that in the course of conversation the name Philippe comes up, all the generals rise and say in unison: "Honor to the unfortunate courage!" Moreover, the participants' lack of memory concerning historical events of which they otherwise boast is indeed striking. For example, General Lenvers de Laveste does not even recall what happened on 6 June 1944, the day of the Allied invasion of Normandy. The play is also dotted with the usual amount of Vianesque linguistic acrobatics. For instance, when Audubon asks his mother for permission to have an afternoon tea for his friends, she asks: "Are they well-behaved boys?" And the son replies: "Oh, yes, mother. They are all generals."[3 6]

In addition, the anticlericalism of the author is well served in this play by the character of Monsignor Tapecul, whom Henri Baudin aptly describes as "a cynical prelate, cunning, vulgar and obese."[3 7] In what Vian considered to be the typically dangerous alliance between religion and brute force, it is he who supplies the generals with a workable propaganda couplet:

> Save, save Europe
> In the name of Sacré-Coeur.

Such words cannot help but recall for the French the famous hymn, *"Sauvez la France au nom du Sacré-Coeur,"* which had known an almost universal success throughout France during the German

Occupation. In addition, like others of his predecessors in Vian's repertory of men of the cloth, he does not hesitate at all to state how easy it is to distinguish the good cause from the bad one by simply watching out for the one that is going to triumph.

But in spite of Vian's characterizations of Army and Church, alienating and perhaps even intended to alienate the conservative public, *Le Goûter des généraux* was, in the 1965-1966 Parisian theatrical season, one of the most successful entries among a host of other productions by more established playwrights. Guy Dumur, for example, wrote: "This play should have been given during Boris Vian's lifetime: no one has dared."[38] The conservative critic Jean-Jacques Gautier, who could not bring himself to write an adverse review, explained: "If you do not have a father, brother or son in the Army as a career, you may hope to be amused by Boris Vian's play. But if mockery or satire about the Army makes you indignant or pained, you should stay away."[39] However, alienated or not by Vian's ideas, there is little question concerning the play's ability to make one laugh. B. Poirot-Delpech stated: "The death of Boris Vian appeared incredible. In fact, it was. After his success in the bookstores, here is one in the theatre: one of the most astounding, craziest [sources of] laughter since *Ubu.*"[40] And Renée Saurel had elaborated earlier: "One laughs to the point of tears [in seeing] the play of Boris Vian and for once the laughter does not spring from any sexual jokes.... The text is somewhat negligent, borders on the cabaret style, but it is always funny."[41] Yet, a cabaret style, even if granted, is not by definition devoid of literary validity. That Vian often wrote rapidly and paid little attention to rigid syntactic procedures are points to which one may easily stipulate. But to say with Freddy de Vrée that *"Le Goûter* is quite a weak play,"[42] appears unwarranted both because of its popularity and because of its laudable theatricality. Subsequent critics confirmed the earlier opinions as quoted above. Jacques Duchateau, for example, wrote: "In September 1965, *Goûter des généraux* is presented in Paris.... The critics unanimously praise not only the play, but also Boris Vian the writer. Jean Dutourd: 'He had a kind of satirical, burlesque, surrealistic genius. This *Goûter des généraux* furnishes the proof. It also demonstrates that Boris Vian was especially endowed, had luster, audacity.' Pierre Marcabru: 'It is proper to recall that Boris Vian is also a great writer. Whoever approaches him is duly rewarded.' "[43]

The laughter-provoking liveliness of Vian's pen is not always profound, yet by his antimilitaristic attitude he indeed anticipates a

worldwide current which established itself firmly only at the height of
the American involvement in Southeast Asia. The darts which he
launches at the military establishments of all nations precede, then, by
many years, the widespread attacks of others who, today, lacking
Vian's humor, are much less efficient than their predecessor. In fact, it
is probably safe to state that great writers, or writers who are
sometimes great, do not merely respond to a prevalent mood in the
public, but rather create it with the artistic means at their disposal. This
is not to say that they are prophetic, only that their lucidity is greater
than that of the majority.

In Vian's case, another interesting example is furnished by his text
entitled *"Le Problème du Colon"* which is found in *Textes et chansons*.
There, a year before the start of the Algerian war, in ferocious language
he *appears* to slip from a political discussion into an anatomical one, by
talking instead of the intestinal *côlon,* the homonym being, according
to him, more directly related to the police and military procedures
vis-à-vis the natives. And then he goes on to say how in the colonial
world "heroism is butchery, legality becomes a caprice, justice is a
mockery, the qualified citizen is reduced to the role of an intruder, and
the one who resists is labeled a terrorist."[44] His anticolonial attitude,
an extension of his mistrust of the military, was thus put to good
litarary use not only in *Le Goûter des généraux,* but in other, minor
texts, such as the one just quoted.[45]

VI   *Summary*

As with his works of fiction, then, the plays of Boris Vian retain his
basic preoccupations: the breakdown of communication due to the
general absence of meaning behind words, present in all four plays
discussed; the superiority of the individual vis-à-vis the rest of his
nation, and all nations, in *L'Equarrissage pour tous;* the shortcomings
of the clergy in *Le Dernier des métiers* especially, but also in *Le Goûter
des généraux;* and the constant and violently rapacious scorn deserved
by the military in all the plays with the exception of *Le Dernier des
métiers.* Such preoccupations, even more than in novels where visual
contact must rely on the imagination, have, on the stage, a particularly
shocking effect which pleased most and alienated some. But Vian's
temperament, conditioned by chronic disease and always pursued by
prowling death, carefree as it became with the passing of time, was
particularly well-suited for the exploitation of suddenly disturbing

impacts. Such an exploitation has indeed a place in the theatre, for it not only arrests effectively the attention of spectators, but it produces, in addition, involuntary reactions and reflex surprises. Admittedly, some of Vian's dramatic themes are dated, but if such responses continue to be appreciated by a majority of theatregoers, then his plays will have a chance to withstand the test of time. For our era, however, there is little doubt about the interest they arouse.

CHAPTER 5

Conclusion

THE foregoing pages have uncovered a multifaceted author, at home in many genres and laborious in many non-literary activities as well. But whether writing novels, short stories, or plays, whether performing in a band or engaging in political or philosophical polemics, Boris Vian always remained a Pataphysician at heart: Pataphysician in the best sense of the word, that is, a person and an artist who is at once destroying and creating. A mocker of presumptuous "isms" even when held by such close friends and supporters as Jean-Paul Sartre and Simone de Beauvoir; an antiestablishmentarian and especially an antimilitarist whose irony does not shy away from poking fun at his own country in some of its momentous historical eras (the Liberation, the Algerian crisis), an outspoken contemporary with respect to his ideas on lay and religious education even though he expressed them a couple of decades ago (ideas which tended to demolish and devastate the status quo in those fields), Boris Vian managed nevertheless to build on the wastelands he helped bring about by a variety of means: his refusal to take himself or his opinions seriously; his practice of intermingling the important and the derisory, pathos and laughter; the subtle suggestion, under the debris, of the imperative of a new hierarchy of values in which man, and man alone, stands supreme, above institutions, governments, and machines.

Of course, Vian's work cannot be said to be that of a literary master. Poetic flights and brio are not always present and, as we have seen, he has had his detractors, whose criticism was, at times, savage. But his novels, especially those which he signed with his own name, such short stories as "Les Fourmis" and "Le Rappel," and plays like *Les Bâtisseurs d'Empire* and *Le Goûter des généraux,* are read and presented respectively even more than at the time of the original publication. Current interest in the works of Boris Vian, at least on the Continent, is demonstrated by the proliferation of scholarly articles and dissertations devoted to him and, domestically, by the translations of his books and plays, the periodic presentation of the latter in off-Broadway productions, and by the inclusion of some of his works in anthologies destined for the classroom. The widespread appeal of the author is to be found, more than in any of the more applauded of his titles, in the general preoccupations of his fiction and dramas: the temporariness of love and life, the shortcomings of all "isms," the frailty of man constantly pecked at by leaders, organizations, and machines; and, above all, the calamity of the presence of disease in all of us, real as in his own case, potential as in those more fortunate than he. What Vian failed to accept, and wanted everyone else to refuse as well, is the process of the diminution of man, of his physical and spiritual assets, of the dignity which is at the core of his definition. Chloé dies, Wolf dies, Jacquemort deteriorates into La Gloire. Time, age, the others, corrupt the zest and zeal of youth, cause it to decay, ultimately to disintegrate and vanish. This is beyond comprehension, Vian suggests, and beyond, too, our will or capacity to acquiesce.

Nowadays, at a time when an author such as Eugéne Ionesco becomes a member of the real Académie and is presented at the Comédie Française; when the previously scandalous Jean Genet draws a crowd at the Théâtre de France; when Marguerite Duras lends her talents, more and more, to the production of commercially successful films; and Alain Robbe-Grillet presumes to be the Pope of the New Novel, one can still look back to the heyday of the literati of the College of Pataphysicians, to Boris Vian in particular. He, one might say, was fortunate enough to die young and thereby avoid veneration and consecration in his own lifetime. In a way (but even more so because Vian's success was almost entirely posthumous), like Sartre who received but declined the Nobel Prize and thereby retained his fierce independence, our author's lack of immediate literary prosperity favored and increased later public adulation.

To summarize, those who uncover, discover, and appropriate Vian, gain part of the upheavals within him, discard the presumptuousness other, more established writers suggest, and retain, perhaps, a human and humane sensitivity hitherto forgotten or ignored. If the writer of *L'Ecume des jours* is, nevertheless, in some danger with respect to long-range survival, it is only because enemies can still point to a certain amount of dilettantism and scandal-seeking in Vernon Sullivan and in some of Vian's articles, speeches, and other activities as the *Prince de*

Saint-Germain-des-Prés. It is perhaps too early to state categorically that readers in the next century or beyond will appreciate, enjoy, and be purged by his more celebrated titles; in our time, however, and in the foreseeable future, indications are that Vian's place in French letters is deservedly assured.

Notes and References

1. Unless otherwise indicated, all translations from French in this text are mine.
2. Subtitle of Henri Baudin's book, *Boris Vian* (Paris: Editions du Centurion, 1966).
3. Noël Arnaud, "Les Vies parallèles de Boris Vian," in *Bizarre* (February, 1966).
4. Quoted by Michel Rybalka, in *Boris Vian* (Paris: Lettres Modernes, Minard, 1969), p. 21; words recalled to the author by Michelle Léglise.
5. David Noakes, *Boris Vian* (Paris: Editions Universitaires, 1964), p. 15.
6. Reported by *Jazz-Hot* (June, 1952), p. 17.
7. Michel Rybalka, *op. cit.,* p. 52.
8. Simone de Beauvoir, *La Force des choses* (Paris: Gallimard, 1963), p. 277.
9. Existentialist terms which point to the necessity of being in and living for one's own society.
10. Simone de Beauvoir, *op. cit.,* p. 73.
11. Speech delivered June, 1948, at the Pavillon de Marsan; reproduced in *Dossier 12* of the College of Pataphysicians, p. 44.
12. *Dossier 7* of the College of Pataphysicians, p. 44.
13. *Ibid.,* p. 48.
14. Speech of Audubon in *Le Goûter des généraux.*
15. *Dossier 8* of the College of Pataphysicians, p. 23.
16. Jean Billetdoux, "Boris Vian," *Arts* (3 April 1953), p. 11.
17. Eugène Ionesco, Interview granted to *Horizon* (May, 1961), p. 12.
18. *Dossier 12* of the College of Pataphysicians, p. 21.
19. Arnold Kübler, in *Ibid.,* p. 98.
20. *L'Express* (7 September 1956), p. 1.
21. Pierre Kast, "Notes sur Boris Vian et le cinéma," in *Cahiers du cinéma* (August, 1959), p. 42.
22. In preface to *L'Herbe rouge* (Paris: Jean-Jacques Pauvert, 1962), p. ix.
23. Pierre Christin, "Gloire posthume et consommation de masse: Boris Vian dans la société française contemporaine," *L'Esprit créateur* (Summer, 1967), p. 141.
24. Quoted by Jacques Gaspard-Dutaneil in *Jazz-Hot* (October, 1959), p. 47.

Chapter Two

1. Quoted in Noël Arnaud's *Les Vies parallèles de Boris Vian* (Paris: Noël Arnaud, 1970), p. 163; source not given.

2. Quoted in *Le Journal d'Egypte* (9 December 1948), p. 2.

3. 1961 novel by Pauline Réage, translated into numerous languages, and for years on the circuit of college dorms throughout the United States.

4. Quoted by David Noakes in *op. cit.,* p. 99; source not given.

5. *La Putain respectueuse,* for example, could only be advertised as *La P. respectueuse.*

6. *Esprit* (February, 1947), p. 14.

7. *Paris-Normandie* (August, 1948), p. 6.

8. *Paru* (August, 1948), p. 3.

9. Jacques Lemarchand, in *Combat* (12 August 1948), p. 6.

10. Robert Kanters, in *Spectateur* (26 November 1946), p. 2.

11. In the unpublished correspondence of Boris Vian, quoted by Noël Arnaud in *op. cit.,* p. 178.

12. Freddy de Vrée, *Boris Vian* (Paris: Le Terrain Vague, 1965), pp. 42-43.

13. See Chapter I.

14. Noël Arnaud, *op. cit.,* p. 196.

15. A famous café in Paris. The author uses a play on words: *mégots* are cigarette butts in French.

16. Provençal word for a special tree whose wood is used to make tool handles.

17. See the article "Our Bobby-Soxers" in *France-Dimanche* (6 April 1947).

18. Quoted by Noël Arnaud in *op. cit.,* p. 60.

19. See below, chapter on *Trouble dans les Andains.*

20. In foreword to *Gargantua et Pantagruel.*

21. Meaning girl or prostitute, companion, door, and bothersome person, respectively.

22. Close friends, *buddies.*

23. Robert Kanters, *Gazette des lettres* (1 February 1947), p. 5.

24. Jean Blanzat, *Le Littéraire samedi* (15 March 1947), p. 2.

25. (7 February 1947), p. 1.

26. Etienne Lalou, *Quatre et trois* (27 March 1947), p. 4.

27. Aimé Patry, *Paru* (April, 1947), p. 23; italics are mine.

28. Jacques Duchateau, *Boris Vian* (Paris: La Table Ronde, 1969), pp. 42-53.

29. Freddy de Vrée, *op. cit.,* pp. 12-13.

30. David Noakes, *op. cit.,* p. 44.

31. Quoted by Noël Arnaud in *op. cit.,* p. 236; source not given.

32. Freddy de Vrée, *op. cit.,* pp. 54-55.

33. An *amour de tête* does not, however, preclude extreme desire for physical contact.

34. David Noakes, *op. cit.,* p. 75.

35. Freddy de Vrée, in *op. cit.,* p. 71, for example.

36. Anonymous, *Bulletin Critique du Livre, Français* (January, 1948), p. 14.

37. Anonymous, *Bulletin Critique du Livre Français* (December, 1956), p. 1.

38. Noël Arnaud, *Cahiers du Collège de Pataphysique* (December, 1956), p. 5.

39. Noël Arnaud, "Avant de relire *L'Automne à Pékin,*" in Vian's novel (Paris: Editions de Minuit, 1956), p. 295.

40. Michel Rybalka, in *op. cit.,* has devoted an entire chapter to an examination of this topic in Vian.

41. David Noakes, *op. cit.,* p. 101.

42. Michel Rybalka, *op. cit.,* p. 109.

43. Boris Vian, *Mood Indigo,* trans. John Sturrock (New York: Grove Press, Inc., 1968), p. 5.

44. See the previous chapter for a brief discussion of Vian's relationship to the Existentialist movement as a whole.

45. Boris Vian, "Chronique," in *La Rue* (26 July 1946), p. 1.

46. Simone de Beauvoir, *La Force des choses,* p. 72.

47. *Ibid.,* pp. 73-74.

48. *Ibid.,* p. 277.

49. Noël Arnaud in *Bizarre* (No. 39-40), p. 150.

50. Simone de Beauvoir, *La Force des choses,* p. 51.

51. See, for example, Robert Scipion's *Prête-moi ta plume* (Paris: Gallimard, 1946).

52. Simone de Beauvoir, *op. cit.,* p. 52.

53. Freddy de Vrée, *op. cit.,* p. 21.

54. The various infirmities of Beckett's heroes and heroines make them little more than partly alive corpses; in *Amédée, ou comment s'en débarrasser* by Ionesco, to mention only one example, a corpse grows in the couple's apartment, pushes them out of bed, out of bedroom, and out of window into the void of death.

55. Jean Blanzat, *Le Monde français* (July, 1947), p. 3.

56. Emile Henriot, *Le Monde* (8 October 1947), p. 5.

57. Georges Goldfayn, *Le Surréalisme* (Vol. I, 1956), 69.

58. David Noakes, *op. cit.,* p. 69.

59. Jacques Bens, Post Scriptum to Vian's *L'Ecume des jours* (Paris: J.-J. Pauvert, 1963), p. 184.

60. Quoted by Jacques Bens in *Ibid.,* p. 184; source not given.

61. Boris Vian, *Je voudrais pas crever* (Paris: J.-J. Pauvert, 1962), p. 53.

62. *Ibid.,* p. 15.

63. Anonymous, *Gazette des Lettres* (21 August 1948), p. 3.

64. Boris Vian in interview given to Gilbert Ganne, *Interviews Inpubliables* (Paris: Editions du Scorpion, 1949), p. 80.

65. For a detailed treatment of the travesty theme throughout the work of Vian see Chapter II of Michel Rybalka's book.

66. Boris Vian, *Je voudrais pas crever,* p. 7.

67. Boris Vian, *Cantilènes en gelée* (Limoges: Rougerie, 1950), pp. 14-15.

68. Michel Rybalka, *op. cit.,* p. 149.

69. "L'Enfer c'est les autres," Sartre had concluded in the play *Huis Clos,* and Simone de Beauvoir had reiterated the formula in her *Deuxième sexe.*

70. On this problem Vian is very concise in the text of one of his ballets which he entitled *Ni vu ni connu.* The stage directions for this composition which transposes the story of Lazuli and Folavril to the medium of the dance, specify that each time the man approaches the woman, the *other* appears; and each time he lets her go, he disappears; enraged, he then kills the *other,* that is himself, but before he dies the figure reappears, unmasked, identical to Lazuli, and disappears forever only when the latter expires.

71. See Chapter 1 above.

72. David Noakes, *op. cit.,* pp. 85-86.

73. Normalians are graduates of the Ecole Normale Supérieure.

74. Polytechnicians are graduates of the Ecole Polytechnique.

75. Eugène Ionesco, *Jeux de massacre* (Paris: Gallimard, 1970), p. 13.

76. Boris Vian, *"Sermonette"* in the record *Intégrale Boris Vian.*

77. Michel Rybalka, *op. cit.,* p. 215.

78. Freddy de Vrée, *op. cit.,* p. 96.

79. David Noakes, *op. cit.,* p. 81.

80. Jacqueline Piatier in *Le Monde* (5 August 1963), p. 6.

81. *Trouble dans les Andains,* the first novel penned by Vian, was published in 1966 and will be considered last in this chapter in order to adhere to the established chronological order.

82. Quoted by Noël Arnaud in *op. cit.,* pp. 246-47.

83. Noël Arnaud, *Ibid.,* p. 247.

84. A diminutive of the word *salaud,* meaning louse, sloven, or dirty person.

85. Michel Rybalka, *op. cit.,* p. 126.

86. See Simone de Beauvoir's *La Vieillesse* (Paris: Gaillimard, 1970).

87. Henri Baudin, *Boris Vian* (Paris: Editions du Centurion, 1966), p. 103.

88. It will be recalled that there was one in *L'Ecume des jours:* the instrument used by Alise to kill Jean-Sol Partre.

89. Anonymous, *Bulletin Critique du Livre Français* (June, 1953), p. 26; for another 1953 laudatory comment on *L'Arrache-coeur* see the article "Vian, le bon Vian" by François Billetdoux in *Arts* (3-9 April, 1953).

90. Freddy de Vrée, *op. cit.*, p. 103.

91. *Ibid.*, p. 124.

92. Quoted by Noël Arnaud, *op. cit.*, p. 246; source not given.

93. David Noakes, *op. cit.*, p. 95.

94. Boris Vian, note to François Billetdoux in *Arts* (3-9 April, 1953), p. 12.

95. A type of congenital color blindness.

Chapter Three

1. See Michel Rybalka, *op. cit.*, p. 59.

2. See Chapter 1 and the discussion of *L'Herbe rouge* above.

Chapter Four

1. For a detailed description of "total theatre" see Antonin Artaud's *Le Théâtre et son double* (Paris: Gallimard, 1938).

2. A useful book on the contemporary French theatre is Michel Corvin's *Le Théâtre nouveau en France* (Paris: P. U. F., 1963).

3. See Martin Esslin's *The Theatre of the Absurd* (Garden City, New York: Anchor Books, 1961); also Leonard Cabell Pronko's *Avant-garde: The Experimental Theatre in France* (Berkeley: University of California Press, 1962).

4. *Les Cahiers de la Pléiade* (Summer, 1947), p. 2.

5. See Michel Rybalka, *op. cit.*, p. 190.

6. J. B. Jeener, *Figaro* (17 April 1950), p. 6.

7. Elsa Triolet, *Lettres françaises* (20 April 1950), p. 5.

8. Boris Vian, in the preface to *The Knacker's ABC,* Tr. Simon Watson Taylor (New York: Grove Press, 1968), p. 10.

9. *Ibid.*, p. 11.

10. Boris Vian, Introduction to *L'Equarrissage pour tous* in *Paris Théâtre* (November, 1952), p. 1.

11. Eugène Ionesco, "La Chasse à l'homme," *Le Figaro Littéraire* (6 May 1972), p. 1.

12. See David Noakes, *op. cit.*, p. 111.

13. René Barjavel, "Boris Vian se réhabilite," *Carrefour* (25 April 1950), p. 3.

14. Mark Beigbeder, *"L'Equarrissage pour tous,"* *Le Parisien libéré* (26 April 1950), p. 6.

15. Michel Déon, in *Aspects de la France* (20 April 1950), p. 9.

16. G. Joly in *L'Aurore* (18 April 1950), p. 1.

17. Jean Cocteau, "Salut à Boris Vian," in Boris Vian's *Théâtre I* (Paris: Jean-Jacques Pauvert, 1965), pp. 51-52.

18. Standing for Claudel's plays *Le Soulier de satin, Le Père humilié* and *Partage de midi,* respectively.

19. Boris Vian in *Textes et chansons* (Paris: Union Générale d'Editions, 1966), p. 114.

20. Michel Rybalka, *op. cit.*, p. 40.

21. Freddy de Vrée, *op. cit.*, p. 132.

22. David Noakes, *op. cit.*, p. 112.

23. Freddy de Vrée, *op. cit.*, p. 136.

24. *Ibid.*, pp. 137-38.

25. Boris Vian, *En avant la zizique* (Paris: Le Livre contemporain, 1958), p. 98.

26. Jean-Jacques Gautier, in *Le Figaro* (25 December 1959), p. 8.

27. Henri Baudin, *op. cit.*, p. 142.

28. Martin Esslin, *"The Empire-Builders," Plays and Players* (October, 1962), p. 31.

29. Philip Hope-Wallace, in *Manchester Guardian Weekly* (1 August 1962), p. 14.

30. Roger Gellert, "Pedants," *New Statesman* (10 August 1962), p. 15.

31. Laurence Kitchin, "Vague Symbols from the Left Bank," *The Times* (1 August 1962), p. 6.

32. Martin Esslin, *loc. cit.*

33. David Noakes, *op. cit.*, pp. 116-17.

34. Henri Baudin, *op. cit.*, p. 21.

35. Boris Vian, *The General's Tea Party,* Tr. Simon Watson Taylor (New York: Grove Press, 1967), pp. 9-11.

36. The word in French is *généraux,* half mispronounced by the actor to make it sound like *généreux.*

37. Henri Baudin, *op. cit.*, p. 125.

38. Guy Dumur, in *Le Nouvel Observateur* (29 September 1965), p. 12.

39. Jean-Jacques Gautier, in *Le Figaro* (30 September 1965), p. 8.

40. B. Poirot-Delpech, in *Le Monde* (26-27 December 1965), p. 1.

41. Rénee Saurel, in *Les Temps modernes* (November, 1965), p. 927.

42. Freddy de Vrée, *op. cit.*, p. 133.

43. Jacques Duchateau, *op. cit.*, p. 221; source of quotations not given.

44. Borian Vian, *Textes et chansons,* p. 83.

45. For a more complete, although far from exhaustive treatment of Vian's attacks on the military, see Charlotte Frankel Gerrard's article, "Anti-militarism in Vian's Minor Texts," *The French Review* (May, 1972), pp. 1117-24.

Selected Bibliography

PRIMARY SOURCES

Works signed Boris Vian
Vercoquin et le plancton. Paris: Gallimard, 1947.
L'Automne à Pékin. Paris: Editions du Scorpion, 1947.
L'Ecume des jours. Paris: Gallimard, 1947. *Mood Indigo*. Tr. John Sturrock. New York: Grove Press, 1968.
Barnum's Digest. Paris: Deux Menteurs, 1948.
Les Fourmis. Paris: Editions du Scorpion, 1949.
L'Herbe rouge. Paris: Editions Toutain, 1950.
Cantilènes en gelée. Paris: Rougerie, 1950.
L'Equarrissage pour tous. Paris: Editions Toutain, 1950. *The Knacker's ABC*. Tr. Simon Watson Taylor. New York: Grove Press, 1968.
Le Dernier des métiers. Paris: Editions Toutain, 1950.
L'Arrache-coeur. Paris: Editions Vrille, 1953.
Fiesta. Paris: Editions Heugel, 1958.
En avant la zizique. Paris: Le Livre Contemporain, 1958.
Les Bâtisseurs d'Empire. Paris: Collège de Pataphysique, 1959. *The Empire Builders*. Tr. Simon Watson Taylor. New York: Grove Press, 1966.
Les Lurettes fourrés. Paris: Jean-Jacques Pauvert, 1962.
Le Goûter dés généraux. Paris: Collége de Pataphysique, 1962. *The General's Tea Party*. Tr. Simon Watson Taylor. New York: Grove Press, 1967.
Théâtre I (Le Dernier des métiers, L'Equarrissage pour tous, and *Le Goûter des généraux)*. Paris: Union Générale d'Editions, 1965.
Textes et chansons. Paris: Union Générale d'Editions, 1966.
Trouble dans les Andains. Paris: La Jeune Parque, 1966.
Théâtre II (Tête de Méduse, Série blême, and *Le Chasseur françias)*. Paris: Union Générale d'Editions, 1971.
Works signed Vernon Sullivan
J'irai cracher sur vos tombes. Paris: Editions du Scorpion, 1946.
Les Morts ont tous la même peau. Paris: Editions du Scorpion, 1947.
Et on tuera tous les affreux. Paris: Editions du Scorpion, 1948.
Elles se rendent pas compte. Paris: Editions du Scorpion, 1950.

SECONDARY SOURCES

(Footnote entries which do not refer directly to Boris Vian's works and those which are not considered especially useful as background material have been omitted from this listing.)
ANONYMOUS: *"L'Automne à Pékin," Bulletin Critique du Livre Français*

(January, 1948), p. 14. Interesting review of the novel, especially in view of the publication's more laudatory remarks eight years later.

————. *"L'Automne à Pékin," Bulletin Critique du Livre Français* (December, 1956), p. 1. Criticism of the novel reflecting Vian's increased reputation.

————. *"Et on tuera tous les affreux," Gazette des Lettres* (21 August 1948), p. 3. Scant, unimaginative review of the novel.

ARNAUD, NOËL. *Les Vies Parallèles de Boris Vian.* Paris: Noël Arnaud, 1970. Voluminous work, containing many insights into Vian's personal and literary life.

BARJAVEL, RENÉ. "Boris Vian se réhabilite," *Carrefour* (25 April 1950), p. 3. Important, contemporary view of *L'Equarrissage pour tous.*

BAUDIN, HENRI. *Boris Vian.* Paris: Editions du Centurion, 1966. Useful only for those already familiar with Vian's work.

BEAUVOIR, SIMONE DE. *La Force des choses.* Paris: Gallimard, 1963. Interesting for the post-World War II background atmosphere in which Vian wrote.

BEIGBEDER, MARK. *"L'Equarrissage pour tous," Le Parisien libéré* (26 April 1950), p. 6. A penetrating review of *L'Equarrissage pour tous.*

BILLETDOUX, JEAN. "Boris Vian," *Arts* (3 April 1953), p. 11. Contains a friendly description of Vian's physical and spiritual assets.

BLANZAT, JEAN. *"Vercoquin et le plancton," Le Littéraire samedi* (15 March 1947), p. 2. A representation of the cool reception given initially to *Vercoquin et le plancton.*

————. *"L'Ecume des jours," Le Monde français* (July, 1947), p. 3. A representative example of laudatory criticism of the novel.

CHRISTIN, PIERRE. "Gloire posthume et consommation de mass: Boris Vian dans la société française contemporaine," *L'Esprit créateur* (Summer, 1967), pp. 135-43. An analysis of Boris Vian's contemporary qualities, of value only to those thoroughly familiar with the author's major works.

DEON, MICHEL. *"L'Equarrissage pour tous," Aspects de la France* (20 April 1950), p. 9. Stimulating review of the play.

DUCHATEAU, JACQUES. *Boris Vian.* Paris: La Table Ronde, 1969. The most recent book on the author, containing an almost complete bibliography.

DUMUR, GUY. *"Le Goûter des généraux," Le Nouvel Observateur* (29 September 1965), p. 12. Brief review of the play.

ESSLIN, MARTIN. *The Theatre of the Absurd.* Garden City, New York: Anchor Books, 1961. Good elucidations on trends and dramatists of twentieth-century theatre.

————. *"The Empire-Builders," Plays and Players* (October, 1962), p. 31. Concise and laudatory review of the play.

GAUTIER, JEAN-JACQUES. *"Les Bâtisseurs d'Empire," Le Figaro* (25 December 1959), p. 8. Surprisingly good review of the play, even though penned by a conservative critic.

GELLERT, ROGER. "Pedants," *New Statesman* (10 August 1962), p. 15. Scant, uninformed review of *Les Bâtisseurs d'Empire*.

GERRARD, CHARLOTTE FRANKEL. "Anti-militarism in Vian's Minor Texts," *The French Review* (May, 1972), pp. 1117-24. Useful article even for those unfamiliar with the texts in question.

HENRIOT, EMILE. *"L'Ecume des jours,"* *Le Monde* (8 October 1947), p. 5. Good review of the novel, pointing to the tragic vein in Boris Vian.

HOPE-WALLACE, PHILIP. *"The Empire-Builders,"* *Manchester Guardian Weekly* (1 August 1962), p. 14. Inimical review of the play.

JEENER, J. B. *"L'Equarrissage pour tous,"* *Le Figaro* (17 April 1950), p. 6. Brief commentary on the play, colored by the reviewer's political views.

JOLY, G. *"L'Equarrissage pour tous,"* *L'Aurore* (18 April 1950), p. 1. Penetrating analysis of Vian's seriousness in the play.

KANTERS, ROBERT. *"Vercoquin et le plancton,"* *Gazette des lettres* (1 February 1947), p. 5. Poor and defamatory review of the novel.

KAST, PIERRE. "Notes sur Boris Vian et le cinéma," *Cahiers du cinéma* (August, 1959), pp. 39-48. Interesting study of Vian's contributions to the cinema.

KITCHIN, LAURENCE. "Vague Symbols from the Left Bank," *The Times* (1 August 1962), p. 6. Brief, sarcastic review of *Les Bâtisseurs d'Empire*.

LALOU, ETINNE. *"Vercoquin et le plancton,"* *Quatre et Trois* (27 March 1947), p. 4. Enlightening review of the novel, pointing to Vian's relationship with Existentialism.

LEMARCHAND, JACQUES. *"J'irai cracher sur vos tombes,"* *Combat* (12 August 1948), p. 6. Ironic review of the novel, revealing nevertheless the critic's admiration for it.

NOAKES, DAVID. *Boris Vian*. Paris: Editions Universitaires, 1964. Originally a Ph.D. dissertation, discussing Vian's major works only.

PATRY, AIMÉ. *"Vercoquin et le plancton,"* *Paru* (April, 1947), p. 23. Appreciative review of the novel, anticipating its subsequent success.

PIATIER, JACQUELINE. *"L'Herbe rouge,"* *Le Monde* (5 August 1963), p. 6. Profound, if brief, evaluation of the novel.

POIROT-DELPECH, B. *"Le Goûter des généraux,"* *Le Monde* (26-27 December 1965), p. 1. A good analysis of the comicality of the play.

RYBALKA, MICHEL. *Boris Vian*. Paris: Lettres Modernes Minard, 1969. Originally a Ph.D. dissertation, more detailed and more up-to-date than that of David Noakes.

SAUREL, RENÉE. *"Le Goûter des généraux,"* *Les Temps modernes* (November, 1965), p. 927. Another good review of the play, appreciative of its humor.

SCIPION, ROBERT. *Prête-moi ta plume.* Paris: Gallimard, 1946. Another slap
    at Existentialism, revelatory of the background against which Vian
    wrote *L'Ecume des jours.*
TRIOLET, ELSA. *"L'Equarrissage pour tous," Lettres françaises* (20 April
    1950), p. 5. Inimical review of the play, prompted more by political
    than literary considerations.
VRÉE, FREDDY DE. *Boris Vian.* Paris: Le Terrain Vague, 1965. Uneven criti-
    cal work requiring at least partial knowledge of Boris Vian.

Index